# BIG FISH

AN ENTREPRENEUR'S GUIDE
TO SUCCESS, IMPACT AND LEGACY

CAROLINE G. NUTTALL

ISBN: 978-0-578-34091-3
Library of Congress Control Number: 2022900020

Cover, interior design and illustrations by Justin Harris
Edited by Carter Dandridge
Proofread by Hunter Nuttall
Photograph of the author by Karson Photography

This book is available at special discounts when purchased in bulk
for premiums and sales promotions as well as for fundraising and
educational use. For details, please send an email to caroline@bigfish.life.

Published in Charleston, South Carolina.
Printed in the United States of America.

First printing January 2022.

For entrepreneurs everywhere who know
they are better than the next Google search.

Mostly, for mom, always there,
no matter how rough the seas.

# CONTENTS

# PREFACE

I'm a big reader. I have had a hand in publishing at least 100 authors, and I'm of the pro dev obsessed variety who have read thousands of books. A conclusion I've reached is that books are entirely too long. So not only did I write a short book for you (more on that below), but I'm going to tell you right here in this first paragraph the crux of this book in just three words: you do you. That's it. If you want to have a significant impact in your career and life, then this is the key, the solution, the message we're going to dive deeper into throughout this book. Lean into the things that are unique to you and do them up big. If you'd like to stop reading now[1], I won't judge. *You do you.*

This book is for everyone who wants to have a more significant impact in their careers. It is for every solopreneur and founder of a small or midsize business. If you are a consultant, speaker, writer, designer, developer, marketer, doctor, dentist, investor, IT specialist, cyber security expert, space explorer, manure scooper manufacturer—any industry, any niche—if you wish to grow your business and have a more significant impact in your career, this book is for you. While I refer mainly to entrepreneurs throughout these pages, CEOs, executives (particularly in transition) and graduates entering the workforce will also benefit tremendously from this book. Even a young

---

[1] If you only read one chapter in this entire book, make it Chapter 8.

tween who dreams of being a TikTok star will gain a massive competitive advantage by reading this book. In fact, there are only a handful of people in business whom this book is *not* for. If you are Jeff Bezos, Elon Musk or Richard Branson, please put this book down. It's not for you.

This isn't just a book about how to grow your business. If you apply the lessons in this book, you will absolutely grow your business, but that's really just an awesome byproduct of this journey. We are after much more than revenue. This book is about tapping into all that you have to offer to create true impact and a lasting legacy.

When I refer to "growing your business," this can also reference your business goal of the moment: getting a raise, landing a job, becoming said TikTok star. Similarly, when I reference "customers," this applies to any stakeholder key to your growth: investors, sponsors, boards, government entities, employers, employees.

This book is meant to serve as a giant shot of inspiration to light a fire under you to go out there and make your dent in the world. As any former party girl with puke and rally experience will tell you, a shot is best taken all at once. As such, this book is intentionally short. It is what I like to call a "cover-to-cover" book, meaning that it is designed to be read in one fell swoop (over a lovely brunch or on a dock with a water view, preferably—environment matters). This is the most effective way for this book to be consumed in order to have transformational meaning in your life. However, if you're a single mom with emotional terrorists for toddlers and can only sneak in a page each night, that's fine too. *You do you.*

I wrote this book because I have come to discover that most people want more out of their careers. Not just more money, but true impact and significance—the kind that leaves a legacy. We yearn for realizing the potential we were full of as children.

When I was little, my older brother told me there was a gravity switch in the house.

My eyes went wide. I could flip a switch to turn off the gravity and fly around like the space people? Suddenly, my small world exploded open to new possibilities I had never imagined. I couldn't believe the adults knew about this and kept it hidden. I was determined to find that switch.

I'm not sure how long I spent looking for that gravity switch... days, weeks, maybe months. Eventually, I gave up and resigned myself to a life on the ground because that appeared to be The Way We Do Things.

At some point, we all resigned ourselves to life on the ground.

We know in our guts that we are sitting on untapped potential. We didn't set out just to make money. We had a purpose to make our one and only mark on this planet. But somewhere along the way, we lost sight of our passionate mission to make way for funnels, scalable systems and a death grip on our bottom line.

We started doing so somewhere near the intersection of The Daily Grind and The Status Quo. The moment we started following best practices. The minute we asked for a laundry list of examples of business owners just like us who have done the exact thing we are considering doing before doing it. We have been conditioned to suppress who we really are and our unique vision for all the things that are generally accepted in business as The Way We Do Things.

This book is for all of the people who know they have something unique to offer. Who know they are better than the next Google search.

You are *not* one of many.

Let's flip the switch...and fly.

# INTRODUCTION

"There is no passion to be found playing small—in settling for
a life that is less than the one you are capable of living."

### - NELSON MANDELA

There's no easy way to say this, so I'm just going to come right out with it since we're in the trust tree together now. We have two choices: Stand out in the Sea of Sameness or drown.

It has never been easier to be ignored. Glossed over with the unconscious, habitual swipe of a finger. No matter the industry, we are swimming in a sea of commoditized competitors rapidly expanding every day as technology, pandemics and other external forces remove all barriers to a vast virtual world. How we are marketing is not only wasting our time and money, but it is making us more irrelevant with each passing minute.

In today's tactic-overload marketing landscape, we have blinders up to the only problem we have to solve: nobody is listening. And the reason nobody is listening is because we're all saying the same thing, which means we're all saying nothing.

Nearly all of us are trying to grow our businesses the same way—by trying to get people to buy what we sell. As we'll learn in the pages ahead, this keeps us blending in with the masses. We're like schools of fish mindlessly swimming around, continuously bumping into the invisible glass of our confined tank. Again and again, with every email promotion we send.

The most successful people in business with scaling revenue, raving fans and massive impact have one thing in common: they stand for something. We have to plant our flag and stop resting on the laurels of our expertise. We must lead with what makes us human, define who we are and claim our unique vision. Only then can we stop selling our products and services and start owning our customers.

Great leaders don't try to get people to buy what they sell. They effectively jump out of the tank, away from the masses, and attract their people by leading with who they are as human beings, their individual perspectives and original ideas. These people are the BIG FISH of the world. And soon, you will be one of them.

This book will fundamentally change the way we think about marketing and business growth. It will shift our perspective, identify the *real* problem we face as entrepreneurs, show us how to stop following the misguided best practices of our competitors and start doing the only thing that really matters. I also promise you a fun read because business books don't need to be boring.

For the past two years, I have spoken to audiences, facilitated workshops and led one-on-one coaching sessions to help shift the way people think with the BIG FISH Framework. I have seen the approach in this book work time and time again in real life from thousands of entrepreneurs and CEOs across countless industries.

By the end of this book, you will think differently about how you are positioned in the marketplace. You will have gained a competitive advantage in your sales, marketing and business growth strategy. You will have a clear understanding of how you can have a much deeper impact on your customers and the world around you. And you will be well on your way to leading a life of significance, creating a lasting legacy.

Time to blow this out of the water.

# PART I

# THE POND

# THE POND

This book is divided into three distinct sections to help guide you on the path to success. The first section focuses on the environment we are operating in as entrepreneurs and business owners. I like the mantra *slap, slap, hug*[2]. We're going to slap ourselves a bit in this first section so we really wake up and feel the pain to which we've become numb. But don't worry: just when it starts to sting like a biatch, we're going to hug it out with the wonderful solution to our pain. This first section is the essential "how to think" part that challenges conventional wisdom and shifts our perspectives. This shift in mindset will ultimately lead into the subsequent sections of the book that dive into the more tactical "how to." Part I, The Pond, shows us why we *must* care. Because I value your time and am not trying to hide any secrets until the end, here's a cheat sheet:

- The current environment is impossible, sales and marketing are futile and if we keep doing things the way we're doing them, we will become obsolete.

- We must stop selling the thing we sell and start owning the customer.

- The only way to succeed in the current environment is to leave the realm of WHAT-HOW and enter the realm of WHO-WHY.

[2] I first heard this approach from Deborah Torres Patel, a Hall of Fame speaker and voice coach. I don't know if it originated with her but I give her full credit for this little gem. Slapping is hella fun.

CHAPTER 1

# I, TOOTHPASTE

*"We cannot change what we are not aware of,
and once we are aware, we cannot help but change."*

**- SHERYL SANDBERG**

Nothing makes me want to pepper spray someone in the face quite like the toothpaste aisle.

You know this dreaded, overwhelming aisle in the grocery store. Hundreds of tubes of toothpaste, all vying for your purchase. It's not Crest vs. Aquafresh, oh no. It's Crest Complete, Crest Deep Clean, Crest Pro Health, Crest for Gum and Enamel Repair, Cavity Protection, Sensitive Teeth, Breath Purification and Whitening Therapy, to name a few. And within each of these categories are sub-categories like 7X Advanced, with Scope, 3D Brilliance, Radiant Mint, Glamorous White, and other such nonsense. Multiply this by every toothpaste brand touting endless choices that are seemingly different and you get the toothpaste aisle.

When the pandemic hit, I was thrilled to shift my toothpaste buying experience online and never have to set foot in that aisle again. Until I searched Amazon and got served up 1,853,421 results for toothpaste.

What the actual f*@&?

Why are there so many options when they are essentially all the same? They all have the same basic ingredients. They all tout a bright white smile and minty fresh breath.

As a consumer, it is overwhelming and straight up annoying to have so many options that are the same. And as the CEO of a toothpaste company? Damn. I'd be up all night every night wondering how I can possibly stand out in this environment.

The truth is, we are all toothpaste.

As a consultant, I get to speak with hundreds of CEOs of Fortune 500 companies, founders of small and midsize businesses, and solopreneurs across all industries about their businesses and innovative ideas on the regular. Every once in a while, I'll speak with someone who is doing something proprietary AF who will revolutionize an industry core to human existence and change the world as we know it. But mainly, they're dentists. Or lawyers. Or financial planners. They all have expertise, credentials and by and large offer the same or similar services.

How is it that we can all be so uniquely different as humans and yet all have the exact same ingredients in business?

Do you know how many choices you have for a dentist? Google says 372 million.

Lawyers? 778 million.

Financial planners? 2.3 billion (with a "B," as in "Boy, I'm in trouble.")

Maybe you're thinking, "Okay, I get it. It's a crowded market-place, but I swear I'm different!"

Look, we live in a world where there are 4 million *cuddling experts*. For realz. Google it. We cannot niche our way out of this systemic and increasingly insurmountable problem.

It's not just that there are so many choices. It's that those choices are indistinguishable. I search for "Essential Oil Experts" and am served up 98 million results. Then I click on the top two leading search. One is Robert Tisserand, billed as "one of the world's leading experts in aromatherapy." He has a blog, education and books. Looks solid. Then I click on his competitor, Jimm Harrison. Jimm is a "master aromatherapist" who also has a blog, education and books in his top nav. And just like that, I'm back to being confused. To me, poor little consumer, these choices are identical.

I remember when Blue Apron first came on the scene and I thought it was so unique, this chef-in-a-box service that delivered precisely portioned ingredients for you to assemble and cook a spectacular dinner at home. A few days later, I got a direct mail piece from Hello Fresh, which appeared to be the same service. Intrigued, I called Hello Fresh and spoke with a customer service rep:

> **ME:** *"Hi, your service looks awesome, but can you tell me how you are any different from Blue Apron?"*

> **HIM:** *"Thanks for calling. We are a meal-kit delivery service."*

> **ME:** *"Yes, so is Blue Apron."*

HIM: *"We take the stress out of mealtime."*

ME: *"Blue Apron says it makes cooking fun and easy. Is that different?"*

HIM: *"We are America's most popular meal kit."*

ME: *"It says here that Blue Apron is literally the 'Top Meal Delivery Service.' I still don't understand how you're different."*

It went on like this until I let him off the hook because there was no answer. There was no difference. Multiply this by the thousands of companies delivering delicious meals to your door and it's not hard to imagine what must (or at least should) keep every entrepreneur up at night.

This problem exists across all industries. I had a very similar conversation with the fine sales reps at Headspace, asking how they were different from the other meditation app goliath, Calm. I got some convoluted version about Calm only working when you log into the app, and Headspace working all the time. Ummm...okaaaay. And those are just the Goliaths. There are countless Davids we'll never hear of with zero fighting chance.

We cannot win a category. We cannot beat our competitors. We may be able to do so temporarily at best, with a lot of money, smart marketing and sheer luck, but we will never win in the end so long as we remain toothpaste.

We'll learn through the pages of this book how to get out of the toothpaste aisle by making the vital shift from WHAT we do to WHO we are. Your profession will make way for your persona. Your unique vision will eclipse your commoditized expertise. We will understand how everyone in the world is growing business the same way, focused on the Thing. More accurately, Thing One and Thing Two: WHAT we do and HOW we do it. This is the losing battle we're unknowingly fighting every day. Once we are aware, we cannot help but change. So then we'll learn a new way, leaning into individual self instead of corporate brand. We will develop WHO we are and WHY we believe what we believe. Shifting from the business to the human is the only true way to win.

Like any good recovery program, the first step is admitting that we have a problem. Let's start this off on the same foot together. I don't have a creepy webcam on you, so it will have to be on the honor system. Please repeat after me aloud (bonus points if you're in a public setting): "Hello, my name is _____, and I am toothpaste."

Once we accept our toothpaste problem, we realize we're only scraping the plaque-covered surface.

We've got to dig deep. To the root. To the decay.

## CHAPTER 2

# SEA OF SAMENESS

*"The universe buries strange jewels deep within us all, and then stands back to see if we can find them."*

**- ELIZABETH GILBERT**

I was standing in a dimly lit parking garage in black lace underwear and high heels, having my Polaroid picture taken against a cement wall.

Once I was deemed acceptable, I was ushered onto a bus to be shuttled to an invitation-only party at the Playboy Mansion.

My 20-something self felt so special, like I had *arrived*. But when I got there and saw thousands of women flooding out by the busload, I looked across the sea of the half-naked and realized I wasn't special at all. I was one of many. Same as the next one. Faceless. Insignificant.

We are all about as unique as a naked girl at the Playboy Mansion, yet we are still trying to market our companies like they are inherently special.

We all sell ourselves essentially the same way. We have a good brand. Check. Logo. Check. Website, blog, SEO, UX, UI, PR. Check, check, check. We all have inspiring core values touting integrity and customer service. We are all posting content on LinkedIn and Instagram. We all employ the same well-intentioned tactics to differentiate our nearly identical brands so it should not come as a surprise that—spoiler alert!—they don't work.

When we market whilst in this Toothpaste Era, we make ourselves *more* irrelevant because we're just adding ourselves to the heaping pile of samesies. We are wasting an incredible amount of time, money and other precious resources in a way that actually harms us.

A friend once remarked that he Googled the best time to tweet. The result showed something like 12:23 pm is the best time to send a tweet on Twitter for optimal visibility. The irony, of course, is that as soon as it was determined and published that 12:23 pm was the best time to tweet, it immediately became not the best time to tweet because everyone in the East was following the same best practice of tweeting at 12:23 pm. The sheer volume of tweets made it entirely impossible for your tweet to stand out. Now, if it was 2007 and you were one of the first people on Twitter, this strategy could work. But circa now? You're tweeting up the wrong tree, my friend.

What got us here won't get us there. There are simply too many people overcrowding every market to possibly use the same old tired tactics to stand out and have any kind of impact.

When we are desperately shouting things like "Last Day! Hurry! COMPLIMENTARY Shipping," "Self-Destructs in 36 Hours" and just straight up "STOP SCROLLING!!!" in our e-newsletter subject lines (none hypothetical, unfortunately), I think it's safe to say that we are officially out of ideas.

More than 306 billion emails are sent each day. Sixty-four percent of small businesses are using this exact same tactic to pummel their audience. Thirty-five percent are hurling their assaults 3-5 times per week. About 50% of people delete us before we even have a chance to beg them for their attention. And we're spending $7.5 billion on this crap[3]. Here's my own frantic subject line: STOP THE MADNESS FOR THE LOVE OF ALL THAT IS HOLY!

We are swimming in a Sea of Sameness. Maybe you're floating along just fine right now, but make no mistake, it's unsustainable. We must change the way we do things, or drown.

[3] Source: Hubspot, State of Marketing Report [2021 Version]. Includes statistics from Statista, 2021, Campaign Monitor, 2021, and Not Another State of Marketing, 2020.

## CHAPTER 3

# THE DEPTHS

"We are here to fully introduce ourselves, to impose ourselves and ideas and thoughts and dreams onto the world, leaving it changed forever by who we are and what we bring forth from our depths."

**- GLENNON DOYLE**

Oftentimes, we end up treating the symptoms—the surface levels of our problem—as opposed to the disease—the *real* problem.

The Sea of Sameness is really just a surface level problem. If I'm a pilates instructor and there are hundreds of other pilates instructors in my market, that's just an inconvenient fact. The commoditization of our services and products is a symptom of that fact. There is only so much we can say about our services and products before we sound redundant. A reformer is a reformer. A tight butt is a tight butt.

In order to fundamentally change and break free into the wide open pastures of business success, impact and legacy, we have to go deeper into the obvious problem of an over-saturated environment to discover the real problem.

We must ask ourselves why the Sea of Sameness is such a problem.

If I own a local coffee shop, who really cares that there's a Starbucks on every third block? By nature of geography, I'll get some foot traffic. By the love of local, I'll get some regulars. Why is it such a problem that it's a crowded market?

You know that fable about the frog? Throw a frog in boiling water and he'll hop out, but put him in first and slowly bring the water to a boil and he'll cook right up. In the Sea of Sameness, we're the second frog. The environment around us has been increasingly bubbling up while we keep doing the same stuff without noticing. We're in a rolling boil right now in danger of becoming crispy little frog legs.

Interestingly enough, the 2020 pandemic provided us with an external threat that smacked us in the face with the real problem because it was so sudden and drastic. If The Sea of Sameness is the water slowly turning up the heat so we don't notice it, COVID-19 was the boiling pot of water that scorched our asses right out of the pot.

The pandemic, and its immediate and astronomical impact on business, showed us exactly how fragile our marketing efforts and sales funnels actually are. An estimated 800,000 U.S. establishments went out of business that year[4]. One third of all small businesses closed[5]. We don't yet know the long term effects on entire industries that were completely upended like travel, live events and hospitality. I spoke with a CEO of a company that sold member-tracking software to gyms. You know, the same gyms that lost all their members overnight. Yeah, he started drinking heavily. When shit hits the fan, which it very

[4] Source: Wall Street Journal
[5] Source: Vice President Kamala Harris on MSNBC, June 1, 2021

much did in March 2020, we become expendable.

Market crash? Nonessential. Disruptive tech boom? Replaceable. Insert any large external shift here and you get the same outcome: Later, gator.

Same goes for the Sea of Sameness. It's just a slower boil so we're unaware. When Google serves up millions of competitive doppelgangers in an instant, we become expendable.

The problem is that the way we run business today is very shallow and wide, as opposed to deep. We do X, and we want to reach as many people as possible to whom we can sell X. We are obsessed with numbers—reach, impressions, likes, MQLs—and scale—how many prospects can I shove into this muffin top funnel?

We go wide at the expense of going deep. This is our *real* problem.

But not all are expendable. The Sea of Sameness simply cleans house, and those that remain are like big trees with deep roots that cannot easily be knocked down or side-stepped.

When we focus on depth of engagement with one customer, everything changes. We become the big oak tree to that customer, and it's going to take hell and high water for them to uproot that. We can still be obsessed with numbers, but different numbers—referrals, repeat business, retention.

Some of us do care about and measure these numbers, but we will never be able to predictably control them as long as we continue to sell what we do.

Depth doesn't come from what we do.

Depth comes from who we are.

And therein lies our *real* solution.

## CHAPTER 4

# WE'RE DIGGING OUR OWN
# WATERY GRAVES

"You can rise up from anything. You can completely recreate yourself.
All that matters is that you decide today and never look back."

**- IDIL AHMED**

This may sting.

This is not a can-do exercise, this is a must-do shift. It's a matter of life and death (of business and potential). Every moment we continue to sell what we do is like shoving a hose into our own mouths as we're drowning. I told you...ouch.

When we focus on WHAT we do, we put ourselves in a box. And we've nailed that coffin so tight that we are completely stuck when a giant competitor, market shift, new technology, or (insert threat here)—emerges and forces us to shift gears or pivot in some way.

Nearly every company on the planet focuses on WHAT they do— the product, service or experience they sell. Paper Supply Co. sells paper. Squarespace sells websites. Wedding planners plan weddings. To be clear, you can be successful doing this. You can be an expert and have a long career, but make no mistake that you are dangerously tied to your WHAT. It is a noose around your neck.

First off, what happens when you become detached from your WHAT? My friend Nick led innovation at some of the world's most well-known healthcare institutions like Johns Hopkins and Kaiser Permanente. He regularly spoke at MedX and other leading healthcare conferences on stages in front of audiences of thousands. He was interviewed and quoted as a leading authority in top medical and business publications. The biggest tech companies in the world always sent him the coolest innovations well before they were released to the public because of his influence.

But then he left Johns Hopkins. And he left Kaiser Permanente. And all of a sudden, he was no longer Nick Dawson, Director of Innovation at Big Important Brand. He was just Nick Dawson. Like so many other successful executives, he had been so focused on driving WHAT he did, that he found himself out on a limb when he detached from his WHAT. Of course it's crazy because Nick is still the same thought leading rockstar, but an event producer isn't going to stick her neck out to book "Dude known for WHAT who no longer does WHAT" as a keynote. I've seen this happen to countless successful executives who stay focused on the WHAT of their company at the expense of developing their WHO as an individual.

In another scenario, say your company is the leading live event organizer in the country. That's what you do; you produce live events. You crush it. One morning you wake up, and a global pandemic has taken live events off the table, literally overnight. You have gone from top of the world to irrelevant in 24 hours with little place to turn. This is not hypothetical. Many CEOs in this industry lost 90% of their revenue in the 48 hours after the initial COVID lockdown hit.

There are plenty of famous examples of companies that got their asses handed to them because they stayed focused on their WHAT, like Blockbuster and Kodak. There are also countless lesser known examples of missed golden opportunities.

I met Patrick Lee, a co-founder of Rotten Tomatoes, at a Meetup in San Francisco. He helped build the app, which was exclusively focused on movie reviews—that's WHAT they did. They grew it slowly and steadily and Patrick and his co-founders sold Rotten Tomatoes to IGN Entertainment in 2004. While the sale price was undisclosed, Patrick openly admits he sold himself short (Tomatometer score: splat). But not just in money.

He says he was so focused on WHAT they did—movie reviews—that his tunnel vision prevented him from seeing the larger ecosystem that Rotten Tomatoes would eventually grow into. If you have a captive audience on your platform looking at reviews of a movie, it's a natural extension to sell that person a movie ticket, which is exactly what happened when online ticketing service Fandango ultimately acquired Rotten Tomatoes and Flixster in 2016, becoming the premier digital network for all things movies. In 2021, Rotten Tomatoes evolved once again, determined to be more than a score by launching its own streaming channel with original programming.

Patrick acknowledges that they missed a golden opportunity and regrets their short-sighted focus on WHAT.

Patrick may have jumped ship early, but the truth is that Rotten Tomatoes is still a sinking ship. All brands are. It may be successful and its journey may be long, but it will always become obsolete in the end because even as it continues to evolve, it stays focused on the WHAT.

Even the most behemoth brands can get knocked down in an instant by innovative newcomers. The likes of Amazon, Netflix, airbnb and Uber have rendered countless "successful" brands obsolete. And the cycle shall continue.

Brands are focused on WHAT, and WHAT is fixed. WHAT will always lead to one inevitable conclusion: obsoletion. When you live in the world of WHAT, you're basically just sailing along, managing your P+Ls, crossing your fingers, hoping that a giant whale doesn't capsize you.

When we lead with WHO we are, it is far easier to adapt and change the way people do, yet corporations cannot. We also inch closer to the end thing we're out to attract, which we often seem to forget isn't a *thing* at all. It's a human.

## CHAPTER 5

# TUBE SOCKS

"The good life is built with good relationships."

**- ROBERT WALDINGER**

Seven days after I had my baby, I ended up in the emergency room with impacted bowels, screaming for my mommy. I still have a hint of PTSD when I walk into my sweet little bathroom. Poop Baby was easily the most painful experience of my life. Coming in at a close second is getting served up Facebook messages from that realtor acquaintance asking if I'd like to buy a house from him...every...single...week.

How many realtors do you know? Countless, if even just peripherally. Realtors have a real challenge in terms of differentiation. The same goes for entrepreneurs in other highly competitive industries like finance, healthcare, legal, consulting... the list goes on.

How can we possibly differentiate among all of the others selling the exact same thing we are? How can we possibly expect to be miraculously in the forefront of a potential customer's mind at the exact moment they need us?

We can't. It's luck. We cannot possibly thrive in business this way while we focus on what we sell.

We can't own the WHAT, the thing we sell. There are just too many people who can claim it. If I sell design services and my customer has 7 billion options for design services, I don't want to pick this fight. Beyond that, as we saw in the last chapter, our WHAT just boxes us in. We become slaves to the thing we sell—we can't leave it, pivot or easily evolve. We can't own the WHAT; we must own the customer to whom we sell.

When I attended the first RISE Business Conference, I wasn't familiar with Rachel Hollis beyond having read *Girl, Wash Your Face*, but attended because of the lineup of phenomenal speakers. When I walked into the atrium and saw 6,000 people jumping up and down like complete lunatics, it was clear Rachel Hollis has megafans. By the end of the 3-day conference, I was one of them.

I felt like Rachel got me. She went way beneath the surface and spoke to my insides. She was completely open and vulnerable which in turn made me open and vulnerable. I never once felt like she was selling me something or pitching some agenda. In fact, I still don't entirely know what her business is, but I know *her*. It felt like she cared about me and worked really hard to understand my world. It was like she was obsessed with me; like she was *my* megafan. And so, despite any initial thoughts I had going in, my emotions connected with her. I liked her, plain and simple. I trusted her because she deeply understood me. By the end of that conference, we were friends. She owned me.

On the final day, Rachel was pulling back the curtain, talking about the power of personal brand and told us, "I could sell y'all tube socks." Hot damn if she isn't right. That's the power of WHO. That's the power of owning the customer.

Imagine for a moment being in the tube sock business. There are 196 million search results, 71,335 of which you can order from Amazon for free 2-day delivery. Could you imagine your measly little marketing budget next to Hanes and Fruit of the Loom? Good luck. See you on the street corner doing a sock puppet show.

But Rachel Hollis could start a tube sock line tomorrow and have millions of dollars of predictable revenue in the door starting on day one and ending only if every last one of her mega-fans moved to Mars (although by then, Amazon will probably deliver there too, so really ending never). Because Rachel Hollis doesn't actually sell tube socks. Or event tickets, journals, or coaching programs, for that matter. She *owns the customer.*

When you own the customer, they will buy anything—and everything—from you.

If we can't sell our customers tube socks, we have work to do.

Lucky for us, we don't have to start sourcing regenerative cotton or creating sock puppet videos in the hopes they go viral. Everything we need to sell our customers tube socks exists within us at this very moment.

## CHAPTER 6

# THE WHOLE ENCHILADA

*"To be yourself in a world that is constantly trying to make you something else is the greatest accomplishment."*

**- RALPH WALDO EMERSON**

Who needs a HUUUUUUG?

At this point in the book, everyone! Rest assured, we're going to start hugging it out in this chapter and begin solving our dire problem.

We know we live in an oversaturated world, can no longer sell what we do, and must own the customer. But what does this really mean?

I saw a billboard the other day with a beautiful, mountainous, river scene and right up front in sharp focus was a refreshing, icy cold beer (nice if you like beer which I don't so, gross). Budweiser? Coors? I looked closer. Patagonia.

Why on earth is an outdoor gear company selling us alcohol?

Because Patagonia isn't in the outdoor gear business. Patagonia is in the outdoor gear *enthusiast* business. And they will sell that enthusiast the gear they wear to go rafting, the beer they crack open at the end of the river, and everything in between.

That is owning the customer. That is what happens when we stop thinking about WHAT we sell and start thinking about the human to whom we sell. We own the customer when we can be part of the entire lifecycle of that person and can sell them everything up and downstream. If Mr. River Runs Through It wears waders, chews on beef jerky, pulls out a fly fishing rod, drinks a beer and journals about his time in nature, Patagonia can and should sell him absolutely everything he needs: the waders, the jerky, the fishing pole, the beer, the journal and why not throw in the pen while we're at it. This entire day, this entire experience, brought to you by Patagonia.

But most of us aren't Patagonia. We certainly don't have their giant marketing and R&D budgets. And we sell things far less sexy like...soap.

It is really hard to develop a relationship based on soap. Hold up bars from Dial and Ivory, and I bet you couldn't care less. It is extremely difficult to build any kind of meaningful relationship on a corporate brand level (Patagonia is an outlier, and we'll circle back to them in the next chapter). You can put the half naked Old Spice guy up on a horse as much as you want, but I would argue that it is virtually impossible to build brand affinity for soap on a corporate level if you aren't #1 or #2 in the market.

But you know who sells us millions of dollars of soap and other nondescript home goods every year? Gwyneth Paltrow.

Gwyneth started GOOP as an email newsletter with lifestyle advice in 2008. Cut to now and it's a $250M company with e-commerce, brick and mortar stores, and a show on Netflix

*(The Goop Lab)* where we can watch Gwyneth and her employees expand their minds with shrooms.

The success of this company is all about Gwyneth, not GOOP. There is a massive acceleration of trust, credibility and brand affinity when we lead with an individual as opposed to the corporate brand. The raving fans of Gwyneth are not just buying soap, but literally anything she sells that fits within their lifestyles—beauty and wellness products, apparel and accessories, home decor, even books and kid stuff. It's the human behind the brand that creates the impact of owning the whole lifecycle of the customer, as opposed to just one bar-of-soap-shaped slice.

We always like to find excuses for why this can't work for us, so let's state the obvious. Hello! We aren't an Academy Award-winning actress who dated Brad Pitt in his prime!

Okay, okay. Let's downshift.

Let's take Ted Dombrowski, my butcher. Ted has a small store in Charleston, South Carolina called Ted's Butcherblock. Ted sells meat. So does every grocery store in America. So do countless meat services delivering directly to your door. So why do I go out of my way to pay more and drive further to buy from Ted?

Because I like him! I trust him. I feel like I'm supporting a human being rather than a faceless corporation with all kinds of profit-centered conflicts of interest. So every week, without fail, I went to buy my steak from Ted.

But things change, and you know what will end a customer relationship with a butcher? Vegetarianism. Or so one would think. A butcher and a vegetarian customer? Sounds like the opening line to a mediocre joke. But nope, Ted was rooted in my life and kept my business even when I became a vegetarian[6]. I wondered what else I could buy from Ted besides meat. Lucky for me, he also sells cheese, pasta, wine[7] and loads of locally-sourced accoutrements. I spend more with Ted now than I did when I was buying his most well-known product, meat. Of course, I'm not the only one. I may think I have a special relationship with Ted, but every one of his customers feels the same way. Whether you know him personally or have simply seen him at the meat slicer in the back, you like and trust Ted and will buy his last jar of artisanal mustard like the loyal fan you are.

We hand our credit cards over to people we like. We'll buy anything and everything from people we like. In the end, we don't actually need much, and we buy tons of junk we don't need, so the WHAT—the product being sold—is deceptively irrelevant. And yet almost all businesses focus entirely on the goods being

[6] I'm too much of a foodie to ever draw a line in the sand by classifying myself as a true vegetarian, but I have almost entirely avoided meat for years ever since reading *Eating Animals* by Jonathan Safran Foer. I highly recommend that every person on the planet read that book to get further educated on meat consumption's impact on our health, planet and humanity.

[7] Since I gave meat a footnote, I may as well give one to wine. In the months prior to the publication of this book, I drastically changed my relationship with alcohol and have Annie Grace's *This Naked Mind* to thank for it. If you are like most people who found themselves on a slippery slope of increasing alcohol consumption through the pandemic and life in general, I highly recommend this life-altering book. Lucky for me, Ted also sells fizzy water and other fun non-alcoholic drinks.

sold. That's not your business. It's not about **WHAT** you sell; it's about **WHO** you are. *You* are what is for sale. The more you focus on yourself as the product, the faster and more deeply you'll own your customer.

**WHO** attracts **WHO**. Humans attract humans. People buy people. If we want to own the customer, we must lead with ourselves.

Most people can grasp the power of an individual, and that's why they hire influencers to peddle their products. One of my friends literally buys everything she owns from an influencer, right down to her toilet paper. *Yes, we live in a world where toilet paper influencers are an actual thing.* The problem with putting your eggs in an influencer's basket is that the relationship the customer is building is with the influencer, not you. That influencer's **WHO** is so powerful that she can run off with her basket full of your customers any which way she pleases. She can create her own product identical to yours, because she already has the customer for it. The influencer has all the power because the customer likes her, not you. You must be your own influencer. To own your customer, you must be the one with whom the relationship is built.

Our **WHO** enables us to own the whole enchilada.

But there's more to the story than our shining personalities alone. **WHO** we are is complex and it's about more than just our public persona. There's another side to this coin we must understand to make the magic happen, and that is rooted in our purpose.

### CHAPTER 7

# SUPERHERO CAPE

*"Knowing yourself is life's eternal homework."*

**- FELICIA DAY**

My three-year-old asks me "why?" at least ninety times a day. At first I thought it was annoying, but now I realize she's completely brilliant (obvi). She gets it. WHY is vitally important.

To understand *why* WHY is so important, let's talk about something I am insanely passionate about: turmeric.

How can you be insane over turmeric, you ask? You can't. It's a ground orange spice. You can, however, be insane over Bill Penzy, founder of Penzy's Spices.

Bill Penzy created megafans when he drew a line in the sand calling former President Trump a racist and adopted highly political slogans, content and products at the height of Trump's popularity. He sounded the rally cry, "Cooking Trumps Racism," introduced a ripped-from-the-headlines Russian spice blend called Tsardust Memories, put together a spice rainbow to celebrate the anniversary of the Supreme Court's decision on marriage equality and did a no-strings-attached giveaway of Mexican vanilla extract to apologize to the people of Mexico and Latin America.

It's why thousands of people are ecstatic to open Bill Penzy's weekly email newsletter that comes with an incredibly personal diatribe about his thoughts on the state of the world, with a CTA deal on a spice to help save humanity, one sprinkle at a time. It's why thousands of people don't just buy his spices, but also his mills, shakers, mugs, magnets and towels. This guy can sell people superhero capes! (Which he does and, yes, my daughter has one).

Nobody is buying turmeric. They are buying Bill Penzy.

Further still, they are buying what Bill Penzy *stands for.*

Our power to own our customer lies in WHO we are and what we stand for, which is our WHY.

Back to Patagonia. I mentioned they were an outlier because in this case, the WHAT (the products they sell) has become stronger and better known than the WHO, founder Yvon Chouinard. This is the wrong formula as we'll see in the next chapter, but what enables them to thrive as a WHAT brand is their extraordinarily strong WHY.

Patagonia's WHY is front and center in the company's mission statement: "Patagonia is in business to save our home planet." Straight up, its purpose is to make clothes, food, anything (a protected park is in the works) that are actually part of the climate change solution.

This isn't lip service. No WHY will flourish unless it is deep and true. Patagonia's WHY runs through everything it does.

Like its beer. The company says the concept wasn't about brand extension so much as applying the things they'd learned in apparel (like their conscious switch to organic cotton and torture-free goose down) to cuisine. The beer is a byproduct of geeking out over regenerative agriculture, Kernza perennial grain and precious soil.

Back in 2011, Patagonia ran a full-page ad in *The New York Times* on Black Friday showcasing its product with the headline: "Don't Buy This Jacket." The ad copy goes into great detail about all the tremendous waste it took to create the jacket and why customers shouldn't buy it. While Patagonia's sales increased 30% as a result, the transparent message was intended to encourage people to consider the effect of consumerism on the environment and purchase only what they need.

It doesn't end with the products and customers; Patagonia's WHY extends to employees as well. Yvon told his HR department, "Whenever we have a job opening, all things being equal, hire the person who's committed to saving the planet no matter what the job is." That WHY is attracting and retaining talent in a world that is constantly at war for great talent.

And it doesn't stop there. Patagonia's WHY also extends to politics. Ahead of the 2018 midterm election, Patagonia became one of the first consumer brands ever to make the endorsement of specific candidates part of its brand marketing. Its WHY also guides all of its investments in protected lands, agriculture and like-minded startups.

Whether you're Patagonia, Bill Penzy or Joe Schmo, your WHY matters. It attracts our customers and goes far beyond business growth into the territories of impact and legacy.

Get ready to don your superhero cape, because we're about to change The Way We Do Things.

## CHAPTER 8

# THE BIG FISH FRAMEWORK

*"When you come to the end of all you know, and it's time to step into the abyss of the unknown, know that one of two things will happen: Either you will step out and land on something solid or you will sprout wings and take flight."*

**- FELICIA DAY**

If life, business and countless books have taught me anything, it is that our problem is never really as it seems. It's never because of the external reason we believe to be true, and so our problem is never solved by addressing the apparent issue at hand. The solution always, without a doubt, requires a shift in mindset.

This chapter is the crux of this book. This is where we shift our mindset.

We think that to grow in business, we need to get more customers to buy what we sell. Wrong. As we have learned through earlier chapters, this was fine back in the day when customers had a handful of options, but no longer works because we have passed the point of saturation. Yet 95% of entrepreneurs continue to try and grow their business this way.

Enter the BIG FISH Framework. Like any good framework, it

is simple, game-changing and core to our fundamental shift in mindset. Also, like any good framework, I first sketched it on a cocktail napkin after a few glasses of wine...

Then I typed it in a simple chart because Serious Business Book...

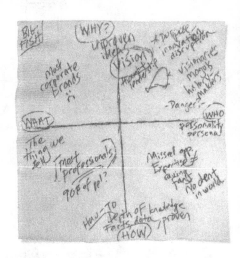

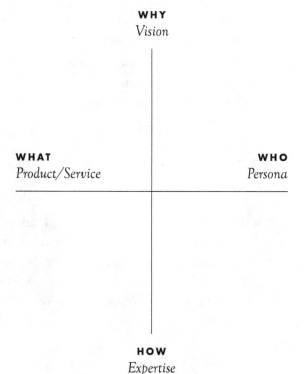

**WHY**
*Vision*

**WHAT**
*Product/Service*

**WHO**
*Persona*

**HOW**
*Expertise*

**ON THE LEFT OF THE X-AXIS, WE HAVE WHAT:**
The product, service or experience we sell.

**ON THE RIGHT OF THE X-AXIS, WE HAVE WHO:**
The individual, the human behind our business, our persona.

**ON THE BOTTOM OF THE Y-AXIS, WE HAVE HOW:**
Our proficiency, expertise, skill, the intricate details of how we execute on and deliver the product, service or experience we sell.

**ON THE TOP OF THE Y-AXIS, WE HAVE WHY:**
Our vision, mission and purpose, what we stand for.

95% percent of entrepreneurs live in the WHAT-HOW quadrant. They focus on the product they sell and their skill to deliver it. That means that nearly every single business you come into contact with on a daily basis is here, doing it wrong. We must stop trying to get customers to buy the product we sell based on the skill we have to deliver it. As long as we stay in the WHAT-HOW quadrant, we are a commodity with countless direct competitors who can also do the WHAT and HOW, oftentimes better, faster or cheaper. We'll sell to customers, but it's transactional at best and a constant hamster wheel of stuffing that funnel. It's a massively crowded quadrant and our only option to fight to stand out is to out-market (outspend) competitors. We all end up shouting as loud as we can (horror flashback to "STOP SCROLLING!!!") but we're all saying the same things because we are marketing the WHAT-HOW, our product and proficiency for delivering that product. Only 5% make it out of here, so this WHAT-HOW quadrant is literally everyone else in the sea. Almost all of us—millions of schools of fish—are trapped within the tank walls of this quadrant, slowly suffocating.

We are trying to differentiate by marketing things that are not inherently different from one another.

WHAT-HOW also keeps us focused on the lowest common denominator. It's kind of like going out to a restaurant in an epic foodie town. We expect great food and superior service; the WHAT (food) and HOW (service) is a given. If that's not there, we're not going to be customers very long. Restaurants don't win on what is expected, and neither do we. If we are financial planners, the expectation is that we sell financial planning services (WHAT) and have the expertise required to deliver that service (HOW). That is the barrier to entry. The starting line. Why on earth, then, do we put all of our marketing efforts behind this lowest common denominator?

The harder we flap our little fishy fins—the more we try to win in the unwinnable quadrant of WHAT-HOW—the more we muddy the waters and confuse the customer.

Let's do an exercise together that will drive you to drink. Let's plot our marketing tactics within the BIG FISH Framework so we can see what's what. I'll do a couple with you and then I encourage you to take a Sharpie directly to this book and plot 10-20 of your most recent marketing activities on the grid. We'll start by plotting some of the common marketing and sales activities. These are all real life examples that have been targeted at me over the past week.

Let's begin.

1. A direct mail piece from a leading real estate company listing the most recent home sale prices in my market, encouraging me to contact them. The WHAT is the product, a house. The HOW is the expertise of buying and selling real estate. There's a picture of a team of people but I don't see a specific person attached as a WHO, and certainly I see no clear vision or mission to classify as a WHY. So I'll put that mark right there in the WHAT-HOW quadrant, closer to WHAT.

**WHY**
*Vision*

**WHAT**
*Product/Service*

**WHO**
*Persona*

**HOW**
*Expertise*

**2.** An e-newsletter titled, "How to Improve Your Personal SEO: 5 Tips for Personal Branding within Search Results." I assume the WHAT is SEO services, although it's not an overt sales pitch. The HOW is the very informative and detailed step-by-step instructions of the actions I need to take to improve my SEO. This comes from "newsletters-noreply@ linkedin.com" so there's not a strong WHO. The blog post focuses entirely on the steps to do this, but never dives into WHY I should care. So I'll put that mark right there in the WHAT-HOW quadrant, closer to HOW.

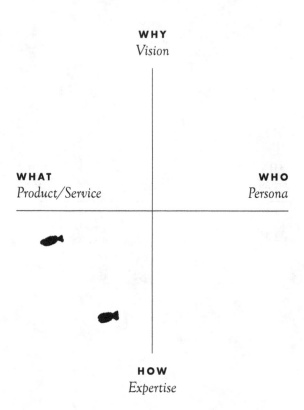

WHY
*Vision*

WHAT
*Product/Service*

WHO
*Persona*

HOW
*Expertise*

Okay, you get it now. Let's go faster.

3. Email promotion: "Back to School...Save 33% with a Quarterly Membership"

4. Blog post: "7 Successful Content Marketing Strategies for Thriving Dental Practices"

5. Email promotion: "Dress for a Night to Remember... Shop Now"

6. Breakout Speech: "Top Tips for Real Estate Investing"

7. Webinar: "Everyday Instagram Hacks for Any Business"

8. E-newsletter: "What's Your Style of Lighting?"

9. Book: "Retirement Planning"

10. YouTube Video: "Top Social Media Marketing Tips & Tricks"

All fall into the WHAT-HOW quadrant.

Now you go.

I'll cut to the big reveal in case you're not an in-book exercise kind of person.

Plotting the marketing and sales tactics of all entrepreneurs and business owners will ultimately result in a graphic that looks like this:

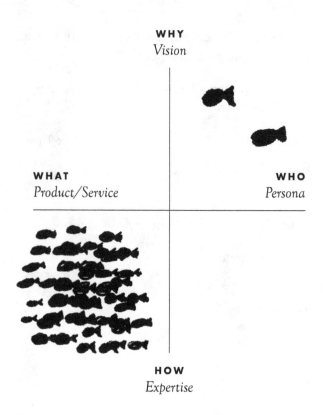

The **WHAT-HOW** quadrant becomes nothing more than a black, inky hole that inevitably pulls us all under until we cease to kick.

The good news in the realization that we will drown as small fish in the big waters of **WHAT-HOW**? We don't have to stay there! We can leap our little fish tails out of that stupid tank and jump across to wide open swim lanes. We must cross over to the realm of WHO-WHY, which is where our value lies. When we live in WHO-WHY—our distinct persona and our individual perspective—we move to a category of one. By default, we are unique because no other human being is the same, nor does anybody else have the exact same point of view or vision as us.

We must shift our thinking. Our value proposition is not in WHAT-HOW. It's in WHO-WHY.

Customers—and I mean *great* customers, raving fans who will buy anything you sell—don't buy WHAT we do, they buy WHO we are. They don't buy HOW we do it, they buy WHY we do it.

To thrive in business, we must operate from the realm of WHO-WHY to attract our people and then sell them everything. We must personify our WHO—our distinct persona—and lead with our WHY—our unique vision. Only when we lean into our WHO-WHY can we truly own the customer.

When we cross over to WHO-WHY, we leave everyone and their mother frantically splashing in the rearview and become BIG FISH.

The current that leads us to open waters of BIG FISH lies in the pages that follow.

**PART II**

# THE
# FISH

# THE FISH

This section is the work.

It's not enough to simply acknowledge the problem. Complaining about the economy will never make you rich. Whining about the dishes will never make them clean (trust me, I try this every night at 8pm). So let us learn from the BIG FISH of the world, dive into their triumphs and apply the lessons to our own journeys. The following pages will help you understand how to leverage yourself and your beliefs to differentiate in our crowded world, own the customer and send your revenue and impact on a rocketship trajectory to an entirely new level. As you develop into a BIG FISH and become better known for your unique perspective and transformational ideas, you will naturally begin building a meaningful legacy.

Part II helps us:

- Realize our WHO

- Uncover our WHY

- Develop our BIG IDEA

## CHAPTER 9

# YOUR FISHY FACTOR

*"The beauty of you is how you wear who you are."*

**- TIMOTHY EGART**

Before you look at me like a poodle about to be thrown into a bathtub, I promise you this next part is going to be fun. This chapter is all about defining your WHO—your persona—which is expressed through your Fishy Factor.

I define your Fishy Factor as a combination of the unique traits that differentiate you from the other humans.

If the rally cry of this book is "you do you," then who *is* you? That's your Fishy Factor.

You must be the face of your company. You must be the product. Just as we define the goods we sell, so must we define ourselves. Because you are the goods, my friend.

Think of your Fishy Factor as a caricature of who you are. It's a dramatized persona that is authentic to your core self. Therefore, in order to define your Fishy Factor, you must start with defining traits inherent in you. There are two sides to this coin: How you see yourself, and how others see you.

Think through all the things that are authentic to who you are. Are you introverted, playful, antagonistic, charismatic? Do you wear jeans, suits, glitter kicks? Are you more of a professor, storyteller, visionary, challenger or comedian? Think about all the things that describe you, from the clothes you wear to what is deep down in your soul. Pretend you're a television writer developing the deep intricate details and backstory of a complex character. Who is this person, this wonderful and mysterious you?

Oftentimes, we can't see ourselves very clearly. Sometimes the things we take for granted as a given part of our personalities are what others see as exceptional. So to get the complete picture, we need to understand how others see us. Imagine how others see you or, better yet, ask close friends and acquaintances. When we grasp how others see us, we uncover our most memorable attributes.

Hone in on the common descriptors. What are the things that feel most true to you? What aspect can you lean into and play up? It could be as simple as your fanatical love of sports, your evangelical way of speaking, your obsession with ruffles or your amazing afro. Aim for just one simple defining factor that is *so you*.

Not to dumb this down because you are clearly high on the brilliance scale if you're reading this book, but if you had a shtick, what would it be?

Think of some of your favorite leaders, speakers, authors or celebrities. We often don't personally know these people, but we connect with their Fishy Factors.

Steve Jobs, the iconic visionary in jeans and sneakers. Joe Pulizzi, the nice guy Content Marketing World founder always dressed in head-to-toe orange. John Cena, the ginormous wrestler with comedic chops. Sallie Krawcheck, the empowering female titan inspiring women's wealth. Blair Kellison, the humble CEO who sends you a box of tea after a phone call. Scott Stratten, the surly UnMarketing guy challenging the status quo, complete with man bun. John my exterminator, the nerdy Sherlock Holmes of bugs.

A Fishy Factor can apply whether you are Steve Jobs or a local exterminator. I don't want anyone reading this book thinking, "I can't." Anytime my daughter says those two filthy words, we mantra it up with the classic, "I think I can, I think I can." *Know* you can because your Fishy Factor is pulled from who you are inherently.

Just start by identifying one element to embrace fully. You are going to eat, breathe and sleep it. Anyone who comes across you should easily be able to draw this association. It may seem silly and one-off, but rest assured, as we practice consistently reinforcing one factor, we will start building a comfort level with our personas. If it doesn't feel right, we may choose a different aspect to focus on. When we are comfortable with this outward expression, we may layer in a few additional defining elements to make our distinct personas really sing.

Think of Gary Vaynerchuck, frenetic entrepreneur, author, speaker and social media mogul. Love or nails-on-a-chalkboard hate him, that man has a Fishy Factor. But it's important to recognize that Gary didn't become the unequivocal internet personality Gary Vee overnight. I encourage you to go to You-

Tube and watch Episode 1 of Wine Library TV from 2006. This was Gary Vaynerchuck's first video blog to promote wine from his wine store. It's fascinating to see a mellow, affable, professional Gary leading us through a perfectly adept, albeit boring, wine tasting of different California Bordeaux-style blends. Now watch one of his later episodes—I randomly chose Episode 304 for a comparison—and you will see with your own eyes the powerful transformation of a persona.

Gary is a maniac (in a good way, as far as personas go). He's insanely passionate, pounding wine straight from the bottle, spitting into a giant New York Jets spatoon, bleeping out his obscenities. He talks lightning fast and refers to the video blog now as "the Thundershow, the internet's most passionate wine program." He no longer describes wines as oaky or high alcohol, but instead, "The Oak Monster" and "I feel like this wine just roofied me." He has disciples he affectionately calls Vayniacs. Cut to today and Gary has an incredibly strong and distinct Fishy Factor. He is unmistakable.

Gary's persona developed over time, just as ours will. We need to be intentional and thoughtful about building our personas now so they may evolve. This is just the beginning of our WHO. And the perfect segue to the next chapter because a persona does not a Fishy Factor make.

## CHAPTER 10

# PUT A BANANA ON THE WALL

"Wherever you are—be all there."

**- JIM ELLIOT**

Dear friends of mine own an art gallery in Charleston, South Carolina. When Robert and Megan Lange opened Robert Lange Studios, they displayed the status quo of traditional southern art. There were a *lot* of mallards.

After scraping by for a bit, they decided to tell the status quo to shove it and started painting and curating the contemporary, hyperrealist work they loved. Marsh scenes gave way to giant clowns, upside down elephants, olives on a stick.

They went on to massive success, gracing the magazine covers of *American Art Collector* and sporting red dots on pretty much every single piece of artwork before they even opened the doors to the show.

Meanwhile, thousands of ducks still hang on gallery walls across town hoping someone will take them home.

In a world that has become so noisy and over saturated, you have to be noticeable.

You cannot paint another mallard.

At Art Basel, indisputably the world's largest fair in the international art market and highly regarded by prestigious collectors around the globe, artist Maurizio Cattelan literally duct taped a grocery store banana to the wall. It consumed the art world. It was sold three times for $120,000 to $150,000 a pop.

It went viral. People came from all over the world to see the banana. Spoofs were everywhere, including photoshopped pictures of Donald Trump being strung up with duct tape. New York City-based performance artist David Datuna pulled the banana off the wall and ate it. He titled it "Hungry Artist."

Ultimately, the installation—if you can call it that—had to be removed from its booth because of the Mona Lisa-like attention it was getting.

Maurizio Cattelan stood out. He forced people to look.

It's not enough to have a persona. Personalities are nuanced and we're not asking our customers to get to know us little by little over time. There is no room for subtlety here. We must be crystal clear about at least one aspect of our WHO, and be okay knowing that it will not paint the whole picture of our complex selves. It is one-dimensional and that's good. It's what makes it easy to grasp.

So be the charismatic growth startup guy who looks like Jesus (Jeremy Epperson). Be the southern good ol' boy copywriter of progressive media (Patrick Rhyne). Be the provocative life coach who says good sex changes everything (Angie Byrd). We must go big with our WHO to give ourselves a bona fide Fishy Factor. If we don't go big, it's not fishy and we'll just blend in. If we don't go big, we might as well go home because we've already become less relevant than unlikely animal friendship memes.

Just as Gary Vaynerchuck took his persona (sports fan, wine fan, opinionated) and amped it into an identifiable Fishy Factor (the in-your-face wine tasting deathmatch guy), so must we magnify our personas to become full-fledged Fishy Factors.

Chances are you know a photographer. There are millions of them (Google shows 875 million, to be exact). Seth Casteel is one of them. But Seth is fishy. He's into dogs. Like, really into dogs. So he started photographing dogs underwater, and turns out, they make hilarious and adorable faces when wet (run an image search for Seth Casteel to see for yourself). Seth decided to go all in on being the Underwater Dog guy. This is a ballsy move because the majority of photographers make their living shooting weddings. Who wants the underwater dog guy photographing her pristine wedding on a cliff in Italy? The wedding photography business is a $10 billion industry and Seth effectively said, "I don't want your crumbs." He drew a line in the sand and immediately pulled himself out of the Sea of Sameness to become a party of one.

He put out his collection of work and called it, you guessed it, *Underwater Dogs*, which became a *New York Times* bestseller (people be cray about dogs). One wet dog led to another and Seth ultimately launched photography books in multiple languages, *Underwater Puppies*, kids editions—like a coloring puppy pool party book—and merch for days (puzzles, mugs, hats, shirts).

Seth made them notice, and now he was at liberty to take them along for the ride. One day, he thought, "you know what else is cute? Kittens! That jump!" So he started photographing kittens leaping through the air and put out his collection, *Pounce*. Guess what else is cute? Babies! Ooosh, I could just chew those chubby baby thigh rolls. Enter *Underwater Babies* by Seth Casteel. Seth ends up getting his own television show, very pleased that he didn't go down the well-worn bridezilla path.

Now here's where it gets a little murky. Seth's success could look like a unique WHAT—the product, *Underwater Dogs*. So often we see success like this and we chalk it up to the product, the WHAT. We can get into a chicken and egg scenario real fast. Ultimately, there will always be a WHAT—a good being sold. It is business, after all. The key is in leading with WHO you are. Seth's product, his WHAT, came as a direct result of leading with WHO he was, the guy obsessed with all things dogs and water. Don't lead with your product; lead with yourself. Your ultimate product is literally a byproduct of WHO you are.

Seth went big on his Fishy Factor to make people notice. So must we.

A friend of mine was a child actor who was directed by Steven Spielberg in a casting session, coming in as runner-up and ultimately losing the role of Elliott in *E.T.* to Henry Thomas (dagger!). In the session, Spielberg coached the kids to play to the back of the room. To go as big as they could, because it's much easier to rein in a performance too big than to pull something out that we don't know is there.

Same with our audience. We must play to the back of the room.

If your customer cannot say about you with 100% clarity, "He's the no bullshit direct marketer" or "She's the Mother Teresa of venture capital," then you haven't pushed your WHO far enough yet.

Are you playing it safe and blending in with the masses? Have you taken your persona far enough to truly constitute a Fishy Factor? Could there be no mistake about WHO you are as a leader?

Fishiness is noticeable. You can't smell like everyone else.

Don't paint another mallard. Put a banana on the wall.

## CHAPTER 11

# STAKE YOUR CLAIM

*"Say something, I'm giving up on you."*

**- CHRISTINA AGUILERA**

Your **WHO** isn't enough on its own. Once you have a strong Fishy Factor, you need to say something. You must share your perspective and stake your claim with your specific point of view. This brings us to part two of becoming a BIG FISH, claiming your **WHY**.

Have you ever read somebody's "About Us" page on their website? I dare you to read ten and see if you can tell the difference between any of them. President and CEO providing valuable insights and streamlined financial reporting...high-touch passionate customer-centric designer...life coach obsessed with helping women unleash their inner goddess power...blah blah blah.

We are all saying the same crap so it makes sense that nobody is listening.

The strongest Fishy Factor in the world won't matter if we're still saying the same old **HOW** things.

I'm the kind of person who reads a book and instantly changes my life. Right after I put down Tim Ferriss's *Four-Hour Work-*

*week*, my autoresponder for checking emails twice daily went up. A month after I read Mari Kondo's *The Magic Art of Tidying Up*, my friend Bryan walked into my house and observed at the orderliness, "Wow, it looks like *Sleeping with the Enemy* in here." And, once a person who preferred her steak rare and topped with foie gras, I have barely eaten meat in the years since finishing Jonathan Safron Foer's *Eating Animals*.

Notice that the author of every single one of these life-changing (and consumer behavior-altering) books says something. They each have a distinct point of view. Tim Ferriss says, "Work less and be a baller." Mari Kondo says, "Tidying is magic." Jonathan Safron Foer says, "Eating animals is whack."

It's time to get the heck out of HOW-town—stop giving proven, practical, tactical tips—and start sharing our individual thoughts, ideas and perspectives. Lead thought around a problem and evangelize a solution. Hone our vision. We have a point of view that is uniquely our own and we must start sharing it.

I recently spoke at a marketing conference with some of the most brilliant marketers on the planet, and I was shocked at the commoditized content coming from the speeches. The lineup was a virtual HOW'S HOW and looked something like this:

- How to Socialize B2B Content
- 5 Ways to Enable Sales Teams
- How to Improve Conversions
- Keys to Webinars that Rock
- 3 Strategies to Drive Traffic on LinkedIn

We know by now that all this content falls into the **WHAT-HOW** quadrant. It simply shows the skill to do the thing. All these sessions give us a list of proven, tactical, practical tips (**HOW**) to execute a thing like improve conversions (**WHAT**). This is tricky because it's a wolf in sheep's clothing. It's dressed up as informative and valuable, but because there is no point of view, it's useless to the speakers who put countless hours into their well-intentioned efforts. Remember, so long as we are operating from the **WHAT-HOW** quadrant, we're in the tank with everyone else.

Similarly, I have seen too many well-meaning entrepreneurs write books like *How to Do Google AdWords*. That does zero to differentiate you. It tells us nothing about **WHO** you are or **WHY** you are here on the planet. It answers nothing that millions of other Google search results can't answer in fractions of a second.

This is where I want to grab people by the arms, shake them for extra effect, embrace my inner Christina Aguilera and desperately belt out her pained lyric, "Say something, I'm giving up on you."

The problem with the *How to Do Google AdWords* book is not that it's not useful. It is useful! It could be a great resource for a potential customer looking to understand how to use Google AdWords, which is of course why such things are created. The problem is twofold. First, if you do your job well and tell them in your book how to do the thing they know they need to do, they don't know they need you. They think, "Great! Thanks for the tips and tricks!" You may be the one who "wrote the book on it," but you're missing a golden opportunity. Because, second, you're focused on **WHAT-HOW** and that means there are millions of other small fish competitors who could say the exact same thing you're saying. They could literally write the exact same book on it. And then, if and when the customer decides they actually need help using Google AdWords, they shop all the options in the WHAT-HOW quadrant, generally on price.

A much more effective and less commoditized book may instead challenge the status quo in search engine optimization as a whole. It may urge, "Call Off The Search" and offer an entirely new way to think about discoverability, which is the reason we even care about SEO in the first place. Defy best practices. Question conventional wisdom. Blow up the sacred cows. Shift thinking around the problem and evangelize your vision for the solution.

When you lead with your unique perspective and vision (WHY), you elevate way beyond the "how-to" section. You leave subject matter experts in the dust on the road to visionary. You shift people's thinking and develop a following for you and your ideas around the products and services you sell.

When Mel Robbins stepped into the world of life coaching, she said a lot of seemingly useful things that sounded like a lot of other useful things out there. She created blog posts like: "Secret to a happy marriage: Put your spouse first." She created videos like: "Feeling hopeless and stuck trying to lose weight? You need to hear this!"

Then Mel gave a TEDx Talk in 2018. The theme was how to stop screwing yourself over and it was chock full of seemingly helpful and generally accepted tidbits. But this one thing she said clicked with people. Mel was a snooze button kind of girl (aren't we all, in secret shame?). She shared a hack she uses to beat her instincts to hit the snooze button. When her alarm goes off, she counts backwards from 5 - 4 - 3 - 2 - 1...and launches her ass out of bed. Of all the things she said that day, this is the nugget that resonated.

People started going nuts over this five second countdown, sharing on social media how they were using this tool to beat procrastination in different areas of their lives. So Mel stopped saying the same ol' and started saying, "It takes five seconds to change your life."

Mel said a lot of somethings in that TEDx Talk. But she listened to what resonated and started saying that something over and over again. The crazy thing is that she almost didn't say it at all. She nearly forgot it in her speech and even later said, "I never intended to tell anyone...'cause it was stupid." The truth is we don't know what "something" will stick with people, but that can't be our excuse to say nothing. It is vital for us to say something and listen. What was it that Wayne Gretzky said? "You miss 100% of the somethings you don't say." Something like that.

Mel Robbins became known for The 5 Second Rule after treading water in the Sea of Sameness for decades. In less than two years from saying something with a singular point of view, she had an international bestseller with *The 5 Second Rule*, became the #1 female motivational speaker in the world, went from facing bankruptcy to making $5 million per year in speaking fees alone, launched online courses and her own live events and effectively catapulted to the billionaire visionary stratosphere. Revenue, impact, legacy. Check, check, check.

Say your piece. Say, "the system is broken." Say, "this is the way." Say, "balloon animals will change life as we know it." Just say *something*. Say something that comes from you. Not from Google. Not from Joe Schmo competitor. From you.

When we get into the habit of expressing our perspectives, people know they can expect a point of view from us. We must offer them a distinct viewpoint from our mental maps so they may consider it for their own. This is thought leadership. It is our responsibility to lead our audience with our point of view. We cannot expect they will listen to us the first time we express our thoughts. We build trust and deeper understanding every time we take a stance and say something that comes from our beliefs. Over time, we become a trusted guide.

Say something, so they know to listen.

From there, we take it to another level. And that level is cult.

## CHAPTER 12

# CULT

*"Oh, Lord, I'm still not sure what I stand for.
What do I stand for? What do I stand for?
Most nights, I don't know."*

**- FUN**

My dearest friend Olivia voted me "Most Likely to Join a Cult."
When I go in on something, I go all in. It consumes me. Defines me.

I was a hardcore game player in my 20s and would quote *The
Rules* at least 50 times a day to my poor, clueless girlfriends
who had no game. Of course they were actually much closer to
a path of true intimacy than I was, but at the time, I felt bad
that they didn't understand how to make men just a little bit
miserable to make themselves more desirable. I was "A Rules
Girl" through and through.

Then I became an "Entrepreneur." To be clear, I don't just
mean I was self-employed. I was an *Entrepreneur*. I wore that
badge like the bleeding heart it can be. That badge sets you
apart from the masses. You are one of the elite few who figured
out a life on your own terms, never mind that you work 100
hours a week and lose sleep over making payroll each and every
week. It didn't matter. This was my identity.

Then I was "Paleo." I became obsessed with CrossFit and eating like a caveman. I instagrammed *a lot* of meat and veggies from overhead.

Next up, "Peak Performer." I got sucked into the industry of brotivation and started consuming as much information and joining as many masterminds as I possibly could to get even peripherally connected to the orbit of The Top 1%. Everything had to become the highest form of efficiency and productivity. There was literally not one minute to be wasted.

I now wear the "Single Mom" badge. And you better believe I'm going all badass and full of pride in that defining label too.

Do you wear a badge? If I asked someone what you are all about, would they immediately be able to tell me without a doubt what "your thing" is? What topic gets you on a rant at a cocktail party? What idea could you push so emphatically that your friends suspect you're in an MLM scheme? This is your WHY.

On a high level, our WHY is our vision. Our purpose and mission and all the grandiose things for the impact we'll have on this planet are wrapped up in our WHY. On a more tangible level, our WHY is an idea. A BIG Idea based on a problem and our solution to that problem. It's a fresh perspective that we bring to the table. It is not a data point or list of tips and tricks that can be Googled. It is an idea that we wholeheartedly believe in and wish to share because we suspect it can help others.

When the pandemic hit, I went into DEFCON 1 full lockdown mode. Seven months later, it seemed I was the only one still there while others had moved on with their lives. Instagram, or what I would come to know as a source of joy-sucking evil post-COVID, would serve me up pictures of happy people on vacations with their friends and family. And all I would think in an angry, teeth-grinding tone was, "must be nice."

A friend went out to a fancy dinner at a restaurant with her husband. MUST BE NICE.

A friend got COVID, lost her sense of taste for a few days, and then was on the other side, unconcerned, playdating like there was no tomorrow. MUST. BE. MOTHER. F@*#ING. NICE.

I wasn't actually jealous or annoyed with my friends. Not really. What I realized was that the parameters I had chosen to set for myself just *bugged* me. The constructs I created simply pissed me off. This was my *real* problem. Because humans run away from pain more than we run toward pleasure, being pissed off is the greatest tool to recognize the real problem. Once identified, it can lead you quite quickly to a real solution.

Which is why one of the best ways I've found to start exploring your WHY is not asking what you're passionate about. Start with what *bugs* you.

What irritates you to your core about your industry? What are we doing wrong? What do you disagree with? What conventional wisdom exists only because we've been doing it that way for so long even though it's jacked up?

What is painful? Lean into what is *wrong*.

Next, we go deep. Ask why 'til you cry. I encourage you to go a minimum of seven layers deep. This helps us get past surface level symptoms to the heart of the real disease. Allow me to reverse engineer this very book, showing how my WHY started with a simple question that bugged me: "Why is there so much f@*king toothpaste??" It looks something like this...

What bugs you?
*Too much toothpaste!*

> **LEVEL 1:** Why does so much toothpaste bug you?
> *Because they're all the same.*

> **LEVEL 2:** Why does it bug you that they're all the same?
> *Because I can't tell the difference between the choices.*

> **LEVEL 3:** Why can't you tell the difference between the choices?
> *Because everyone says the same shit.*

> **LEVEL 4:** Why does everyone say the same shit?
> *Because they are talking about things that are not inherently different.*

> **LEVEL 5:** Why are they talking about things that are not inherently different?
> *Because they are talking about the wrong things. (This is the level where you usually get to the good stuff.)*

> **LEVEL 6:** Why are they talking about the wrong things?
> *Because they don't know what else to say.*

**LEVEL 7**: Why don't they know what else to say?

*Because they haven't been given a new way to think.*

End scene.

Digging deeper into what bugs us ultimately leads us on a journey to develop solutions and ideas that are fundamental to our purpose in business and life.

Once we discover what bugs us and dig to the depths of it to uncover the real problems and solutions, we stake our claim.

Jay Acunzo is really good at asking why, which has been the catalyst for his entrepreneurial journey. Jay started as a sports writer, cutting his teeth at Hartford Courant and ESPN, moving to tech companies Google and Hubspot, landing at seed stage investment company Nextview Ventures. All along, Jay kept a blog called Sorry for Marketing where he shared his thoughts on content marketing and creating quality, craft-driven work.

One day, Jay wrote a blog post. It was titled: "The One Secret Thing All Successful People Do." A quick scroll reveals the body content: "They don't look for secrets to success in freaking blog posts."

That's it. One sentence. Well, this little piece of content goes viral. This sends Jay into an existential meltdown. Here's a guy who has dedicated his career to producing quality content and this spoof post—one that makes fun of all the crappy click-bait content that exists—is his most successful piece as a writer.

WTF.

This is when Jay starts asking why. His first question is, "Why does content marketing suck?"

He launches a podcast called Unthinkable to openly explore the deep layers of his dig. He quickly lands on the hypothesis that hacks, and our obsession with shortcut culture, is the problem. But he keeps on digging.

He asks, "Why is shortcut culture a problem?" He dives into his next question with full gusto, speaking with people at conferences, clients and other content marketers. He realizes that shortcut culture leads us all to follow best practices. This must be the issue.

He goes a layer deeper asking, "Why are best practices an issue?" I mean, they are *best* for a reason, am I right? No, turns out I'm not right. Because the second we all start following the same best practices, they cease to be the best and start to be the average.

Jay realizes that the real problem is not in bad content or hacks or best practices—these are merely symptoms. The real epidemic is that it has never been easier to be average. Jay sets out to bridge the gap between what data says worked and what intuition says could work.

He asked why 'til he cried and it led him to his vision.

Jay stands for trusting your intuition to be more creative in business. He was named a Top 50 Marketing Influencer and his podcast is top-ranked for entrepreneurs and creatives. He went from making $0 speaking to five figures per gig. He published his first book and was able to leave his day job to become a full-time speaker, host, and complete rockstar. Jay is beyond just dollars and cents. I've seen grown men cry during his keynote and tweets like "speaking to my soul" and "mind blowingly inspired" are the norm. Jay is making a true impact on people's lives.

I've always loved the lyrics of Fun's *Some Nights*, and it turns out, this is the only question we need to ask ourselves to define our WHY:

What Do I Stand For?

Not "what do I do" or "what can I sell" or "what is my value proposition."

What do I stand for?

This is our WHY, our mission, our vision. This WHY is our 7-layer-dip purpose, and it's everything. We must plant an intentional flag and own it.

But purpose can be a bit pie in the sky. We've got to bring it down to earth. How do we distill what we stand for into a bite-sized, tangible thing that can be embraced and consumed? Enter our BIG Idea.

## CHAPTER 13

# YOUR BIG IDEA

*"The journey of a thousand miles begins with one step."*

**- LAO TZU**

This chapter helps us get more tangible with our BIG Idea, which serves as our presenting solution as a BIG FISH.

If my purpose (WHY) is to get people to differentiate themselves and break free from the masses, my solution is for them to stop focusing on their products and start amplifying their personas. The concept of being a BIG FISH—and the framework in Chapter 8—literally becomes *my* BIG Idea.

When things get hard, people tend to gloss over, so please do not get glossy here! Successful leaders do not skip this step. They built multi-million and billion-dollar businesses by staking their claims in a BIG idea powered by their WHO and WHY.

Let's circle back to Mel Robbins. She has her WHO and WHY— she is a persuasive, no nonsense lawyer-turned-motivational speaker on a mission to save people from self-sabotage—but the star that shined was her BIG Idea, "The Five Second Rule." This was her point of view on a silver platter. She was saying, "You are procrastinating your life away. You can change the entire trajectory of your life in 5 seconds. Do it with this 5 Second Rule." Your BIG Idea is your presenting solution that enables your audience to experience your **who** and **why** in a nice, digestible package. It is the byproduct of your **who-why**. When we look at the success of Mel's 5 Second Rule, we could mistake it for a unique product (**what**) if we didn't know any better. There *is* a **what**. The book, the speech, the online course, the app—each one is a product being bought. But "The 5 Second Rule" itself is not a **what**. It is a BIG Idea that Mel imagined into existence. And it's the reason all of the products are being bought. We must grasp that the product being bought has very little to do with **what** the product is. In this case, it has everything to do with Mel's unique perspective and original idea. We like her, we trust her, we buy into her solution for our life, whatever that is. Even though Mel has now successfully productized "The 5 Second Rule," it's not a **what**. It's a BIG Idea that comes from Mel and Mel only. There are no limits to our BIG Ideas. In fact, Mel is onto her next BIG Idea with "The High 5 Habit."

Gary Keller built Keller Williams on his Millionaire Real Estate Agent formula. Elisabeth Kübler-Ross revolutionized the psychiatry industry with the Five Stages of Grief. Jane Nelsen saved countless spanked bottoms with her Positive Discipline parenting approach. None of these are the **what**, the products being sold. These are all BIG Ideas. In fact, you can trace almost every single highly successful leader back to what I would consider a truly BIG Idea—a solution based on the individual's unique perspective and creative vision.

Developing a BIG Idea can be daunting. The goal here is not necessarily for you to walk away with a million-dollar idea (although that would be nice and yes, I'll totally accept an invitation to your future home on the Amalfi Coast), but to simply start thinking big and flexing the muscle of staking your claim in something. At this point, we know we need to say something. What are we going to say? We know we need to stand for something. What are we going to stand for? How do we convey that as a concrete idea?

Start throwing some spaghetti at the wall and see what sticks.

Are you a hairstylist? Stop running Groupons (#tbt) and refer-a-friend discounts that nobody uses because no one wants to ask her colleague to get his hair cut at your salon so she can get $15 off next time. Instead, think like Devachan Salon founder Lorraine Massey who created a cult following with her Curly Girl Method (her BIG Idea) and subsequent DevaCurl product line. The moment I read Lorraine's Curly Girl Handbook, a.k.a. the Bible for curly hair, you better believe I threw out all my hair dryers, flat irons and shampoos, ordered all the DevaCurl products and ditched my hairstylist in search of a DevaCurl-certified salon. And when Lorraine sold that company, I followed her right on over to her new CurlyWorld line. In a field where there are more than half a million hairdressers to choose from, Lorraine created loyal disciples around the globe because she *stands for* curly hair empowerment, which she expressed through her BIG Idea, the Curly Girl Method.

Are you a book publisher? Instead of competing with the 2 billion book publishing results on Google, think like Adam Witty who coined the term "Authority Marketing." Adam effectively leapt out of the Sea of Sameness and moved to a category of one with this move. Instead of a publisher pedaling books on price, he began to educate CEOs and their marketing teams on an entirely new business growth strategy focused on systematically building authority for CEOs to serve as on-ramps back to their businesses. Instead of writing a book about how to publish a business book, he wrote the book on Authority Marketing. He gives speeches and leads webinars on Authority Marketing. He launched the Authority Marketing podcast. Adam sells books, but he doesn't concern himself with selling books. He just keeps amplifying his vision for Authority Marketing, his BIG Idea. As a result, Adam sells his services for up to 10 times the revenue of other hybrid publishers offering similar services.

Venture capitalist? Think like Greg Shepard who developed BOSS, the Business Operating Support System. This is not a product; it's a BIG Idea. In an effort to drive deal flow and help entrepreneurs overcome the disheartening statistic that 95% of startups fail, Greg created the BOSS methodology based on the 100% success rate he has had over the past 20 years starting 12 companies and exiting each one within 24-36 months. He is amplifying his BIG Idea with a book, *Meet the BOSS: The Agile Playbook for Growth Companies*. And The BOSS Podcast. And every platform where Greg can share his BIG Idea of a new kind of operating system for startups. With his BIG Idea, he's no longer just "the money," but an ardent guide for entrepreneurs.

These are not overnight ideas. We will need to develop our BIG Ideas in public (more on this in the next section). Becoming a BIG FISH is an iterative process, and we must be willing to air our dirty (imperfect) laundry, listen to feedback or new findings, and adjust our presenting solutions accordingly.

This is all industry-agnostic. No matter the field, there is always a slice we can carve out as our own. There is always a perspective we can have that is totally unique to our vision. No excuses.

It's time for us to step into the realm of **WHO-WHY**. Embrace your individual persona, unique perspective and original ideas.

At this point, we understand "The Pond"—the world we live in—and why focusing on our products and expertise to grow business is untenable. We know we need to get away from all the other schools of fish in the grueling tank of **WHAT-HOW** and leap over to become BIG FISH in the realm of **WHO-WHY**. We grasp "The Fish"—our **WHO** (our distinct persona, our Fishy Factor) and **WHY** (our vision, what we stand for). We may even have an inkling of an idea or a starting place to begin imagining our BIG Idea, the tangible solution that expresses our **WHO** and **WHY**. All that is left is sharing it with the world. This leads us into our final section, "The Swim."

# THE SWIM

# THE SWIM

Here we are in the final section of the book. This last section is all about sharing our WHO-WHY with the world. We must put our WHO-WHY out there if we want to leverage it to grow the backend of our businesses, have social impact, and create a personal legacy. Without The Swim, there is no effect. In fact, I have a sneaking suspicion that as CEOs, entrepreneurs and business leaders, most of us actually have a fairly strong sense of our WHO and WHY. We simply do not share it. We do not *lead* with it. So there is no effect. Therefore, in many ways, this is the most important section of the book—giving our WHO-WHY the chance to be heard so it may have an impact. Part III, The Swim, helps us:

- Simplify our message to maximize its impact

- Tap into our own humanity

- Recognize the three fears that will stop us from being successful

- Recognize the one big danger to avoid when we do become BIG FISH

- Feel empowered to actually make this fundamental shift in our businesses and lives

## CHAPTER 14

# SIMPLIFY TO AMPLIFY

"Success isn't that difficult; it merely involves taking twenty steps in a singular direction. Most people take one step in twenty directions."

**- BENJAMIN HARDY**

Our attention spans are not as short as marketing myths would have us believe. Any species that can binge a year-long Netflix series in a day does not have an attention span problem.

We have an attention *grab* problem.

We have perfect customers out there who have no idea that they should pay attention to us because we blend into the increasingly assaulting noise they actively tune out.

Even when we manage to grab their attention, we often lose it either immediately or when something better comes along because we're competing with ourselves, bombarding them with too many messages, leaving them a tad unsure or downright confused. And just like that, they're gone.

The only way to stand out in today's impossible world is to simplify everything down to your one thing. Your WHO-WHY. The thing you stand for. Your one BIG Idea. And then GO BIG with it. Take it ALL THE WAY.

The hardest part about simplifying is that of which we must let go. We tend to fall in love with our ideas and hold onto our messages like a hoarder terrified to clean out our closets for fear that we may need those exact paint-splattered cut off jean shorts one day when we decide to wash our car for nostalgia's sake. You get it.

We must let go of everything else but our WHO-WHY, or tactically, our BIG Idea. Everything else just dilutes it to the point that it is no longer BIG FISHY. It's just a little something in the sea of somethings we do and then we're right back to being indiscernible small fish.

Larry Smith was a magazine publisher. Day after day, Larry would give it everything he had to create compelling content for Smith Magazine, get more readers, secure advertising dollars to keep it all afloat. Of course our society has no shortage of media outlets all doing the exact same thing, stretching limited reader attention and advertising dollars so thin that if you're ever lucky enough to get a piece of that juicy pie, it's more like a diet cracker made of air that disintegrates before you can even taste it. Larry's reader growth was stagnant. He left countless messages for potential advertisers who never called him back. Larry was treading water in the Sea of Sameness. Exhaustion loomed.

One day, Larry hears that Ernest Hemingway was once challenged to write a story in six words. Legend has it the story goes, *"For Sale: Baby shoes, never worn."* Woah. Dark. Larry decides it's a good time to solicit some user-generated content, posts the challenge to readers to write their own story in six words, shuts off his computer and goes to bed. The next morning, he has 7,000 emails in his inbox from readers. They are filled with hope ("I'm going to change the world") and pain ("Dear Memory, you are fading fast"). They are funny, sad, inspirational. Most importantly, they are there. This is by far the most traction Larry has had with any piece of content in the history of his magazine.

What's amazing about Larry's story is not that this stroke of luck happened. Because at this point, we can call it luck. It could still be a flash in the pan. It's what Larry does from here that creates true impact.

Larry decides to go all in. He boldly puts all of his chips on the table. He brands this experiment: "Six-Word Memoirs, a project of Smith." He kills every other piece of typical (average) content filling his publication and website—news, calendar of events, restaurant reviews, brushes with fame, features like Beautiful Pregnant Women. He revamps everything around Six Words and trademarks the tagline: "One Life. Six Words. What's Yours?" He partners with the young co-founders of a startup called Twitter to launch a Six-Word Festival. He continues to add fuel to the fire and strips away all the other stuff that burns but ultimately burnt out and simply smothered the flame. Pretty soon, celebrities start sharing their six-word memoirs:

Stephen Colbert:
*"Well I thought it was funny."*

Malcolm Gladwell:
*"Father: 'Anything but journalism.' I rebelled."*

Sarah Silverman:
*"Said vagina more than necessary. Vagina."*

Larry takes Six-Word Memoirs into schools. Kids write adorable and poignant things like, "Chipotle will never love me back." He launches live open mic events inviting readers to come share the stories behind their six words.

Remember all those potential advertisers who never called Larry back because he was one of many magazine publishers? Now they're approaching him because he is *the* Six-Word Memoir guy. Mini Cooper creates ad campaigns off of six-word submissions. Honest Tea Company features the six-word memoirs of famous people on the underside of its bottle caps. And they pay him big, juicy pie money. None of this fat free crap.

Larry doesn't stop there. He keeps going all in on his *one* thing, amplifying and leveraging it for all it's worth. Enter: products! That alluring passive revenue that stays as a mirage for so many entrepreneurs trudging through the desert. Larry launches six-word t-shirts (now you can pass someone on the street and know they believe that "silent auctions and alcohol don't mix"), calendars (beware the date that "ex-wife and contractor now have house." Ouch), board games, and books. Countless books. Each one filled with six-word stories on a topic like work, love and heartbreak, the teenage years, immigration, and Jewish life. Larry can keep niching these out forever, and it's all user-generated content, making it a renewable and endless churning machine.

Now, Larry travels the world and speaks on stages (usually wearing a t-shirt that says something like, "Threw spaghetti at wall. Some stuck.") inspiring audiences with the story of how he sparked a global phenomenon with six words.

As a former magazine publisher myself who scratched and clawed for local ad dollars, I am blown away (a.k.a. mad jealous) by the beautiful and powerful simplicity of what Larry did with Six-Word Memoirs. His success came from his commitment to let go of everything else but his one thing that was working. He simplified to amplify the hell out of it. In doing so, he not only gained the audience and revenue he was initially after, but had a far greater impact on the millions of people he inspired to distill their own lives, goals and dreams down to six words. In the course of his journey, Larry went from a typical toothpaste-y, forgotten-when-distribution-stops magazine publisher to the one guy who will always be remembered for his Six-Word Memoirs.

We must simplify our BIG Idea to make the message clear and meaningful.

Let's sum this up in, say, six words:

Revenue, impact, legacy. Simplify to amplify.

In the spirit of simplifying, we can go ahead and simplify everything we've learned to this point including our prescription for success in another six words:

Lead with what makes you human.

## CHAPTER 15

# I, HUMAN

*"We don't need more stuff. We need more humanity."*

**- SETH GODIN**

This is a ballsy thing to say since my dad is a retired mathematician, but I don't care a lick about my daughter learning math. I care much more about the other skills she will develop through the act of learning math, but the math itself is irrelevant. Computers can do it, which means that skill does not make us valuable. Swap in a whole lot of other WHATS and HOWS and you get this exact same scenario.

I was at ORDCamp, an un-conference in Chicago full of geek-turned-baller tech futurists, and was speaking with Dropbox's Chief Technology Officer about this very subject. We speculated how massively different the world will look in 20 years when my daughter enters it as an adult, and contemplated what value she will bring in that landscape. Here's the verdict: We will no longer add any value whatsoever in the WHAT-HOW space. Technology will own it. If we stay in this realm, we will be obsolete. At best, we'll lose our jobs or companies. At worst, we will grapple with our worth as human beings. I'm not saying this in a, "we're all screwed, so let's just eat more ice cream" kind of way, but we need to actively position ourselves knowing that this new reality is rapidly approaching. Our currency and value will exist *only* in the things that make us uniquely human, and that is in the WHO-WHY realm.

Yet we continue day after day running the frantic race of WHAT-HOW with blinders on, attempting to systematically improve our sales and marketing, business and profit.

It's easy to understand why the Software as a Service model is an entrepreneur's wet dream. SaaS, the "on demand" software licensing subscription model, is systematic, scaleable, and devoid of unpredictable variability. We are all trying to create this model in some way within our own industries. Everyone is trying to aaS it up. There's AIaaS (Artificial Intelligence as a Service), KaaS (Knowledge as a Service), PaaS (Platform as a Service), DRaaS (Disaster Recovery as a Service). It's a big aaS list. With XaaS (Everything as a Service), it's actually infinite. While we continue to make leaps and bounds in the race to optimize technology, we must recognize that our achievements are forcibly changing the value we provide to the world. The aaS model is straight up obsolescence by design. Talk about a can of whoop-aaS. (Okay, I'll stop now).

A brand is not human. Systems, taglines, product features and beautifully optimized apps are not human. A listicle of how-to instructional tips is damn well not human. We have knowledge, but so does Wikipedia. We can research, but so can Google. And we don't stand a chance against the infinite scale of these systems.

We must focus on the things that make us *uniquely* human. Humans are passionate. We are critical thinkers who can lead new thought with our strong opinions and original ideas. We have mission-driven vision.

The things that enable us to thrive when our world goes bananas—whether we are faced with millions of lookalike competitors on Google, a global pandemic, an economic downturn, or when 90% of workplace functions are automated—are the things that make us uniquely human, our WHO and our WHY. They are the things that enable us to thrive no matter what our world looks like, and they are each interpreted in a unique way within each individual, which is exactly what makes you—I'm talking to YOU personally, unique human—irreplaceable. If two people solve a math equation, the solution is the same. If two people think up a new vision for a business solution, you'll have two totally different visions.

There is no real complexity here. If you've gotten into the weeds of your thoughts around your Fishy Factor or BIG Idea, zoom out. Simply lead with what makes you human.

I think we all intuitively know this—that leading with our humanity is the right way. Yet we stay stuck. Let's talk about why. In the next three chapters, I address the most common fears that keep us firmly planted in WHAT-HOW and will stop us in our tracks from becoming BIG FISH.

You may want to sit down. This first one is a doozy.

## CHAPTER 16

# W.K.Y.S.

*"To live a creative life, we must lose our fear of being wrong."*

**- JOSEPH CHILTON PEARCE**

I once got into a heated discussion with a 13-year-old on an airplane over Edward versus Jacob. I was a real Twihard. As in, I was gifted a lifesize cardboard cutout of Edward Cullen from the Twilight series for my 30th birthday level Twihard.

My fangirl status transitioned to the actor himself, Robert Pattinson, and I decided I needed to meet him in real life to see that he was not all that I imagined him to be so I could get over my crush and return to my normal life.

I called a producer I knew at *The Tonight Show* from my days as a Hollywood publicist and asked if she could let me know the next time Robert Pattinson was scheduled to be on the show so I could fly out to L.A. and hang out in the green room to casually meet him.

After a stunned beat she said, "Is this Caroline...*Nuttall?*"

"Yes," I replied.

"The same Caroline Nuttall who used to be a publicist at BWR is now calling me for information to stalk a celebrity?" she asked incredulously.

I waited.

"So, that's a no then?" I asked. She hung up.

I've only fangirled over one other person—in a much more appropriate way—and that is Andrew Davis, speaker, author and one of the most influential marketers on the planet. I first saw Andrew give a keynote speech and changed my entire business model overnight based on his talk. Over the years, he became my mentor, colleague and friend. I will always be in awe of Andrew's big thinking vision and his ability to fundamentally shift the way people see things. Out of an endless sea of "thought leaders," he *actually* leads thought. Simply put, he's brilliant, and in a completely enthusiastic, curious, unpretentious way.

When he submitted his manuscript for his first book, *Brandscaping,* his editor returned it thoroughly marked up as any good editor will do. Alongside the slashes and suggestions, the letters "W.K.Y.S." were scribbled in the margins throughout.

Andrew tried to think through possible word combinations "W.K.Y.S." could stand for. He Googled "W.K.Y.S." only to find a local radio station. He looked up short form abbreviations from AP-style editor notes to no avail.

He and his editor had a meeting a few days later. By then, Andrew had racked his brain over the possible meaning of these four little letters.

"What did you think of the edits?" his editor asked him.

"They're great, thank you! I just have one question that has been keeping me up for days. What in the world is W.K.Y.S?" he asked.

"It means, 'We Know You're Smart,'" she answered. "You don't need to prove it."

Y'all. *Woah.* This is a giant flashing neon warning sign.

W.K.Y.S. is what will stop every last one of us in our tracks en route to BIG FISHdom. Our natural instinct will be to keep our ideas to ourselves for fear others may think they're dumb, or muddy them up with endless data and so many proof points that our fresh thinking gets lost. Our default will be to continue sharing only what we know for certain so people can go on thinking we're brilliant. If you think this won't happen to you, think again. If humble-pie-smarty-pants Andrew Davis can fall prey to W.K.Y.S., anyone can.

The truth is that deep down, we are scared to leave our WHAT-HOW comfort zone. WHAT is safe. WHAT is not personal, whereas WHO is deeply personal. HOW is concrete. Knowledge and proficiency are learned, and it is widely accepted that our years of experience validate our expertise. Whereas our WHY—our perspective, our vision—may be challenged and we don't have all the data to back it up. Someone may disagree with our point of view. When we are in the realm of WHO-WHY, we are terrified to be vulnerable in any way that potentially threatens our perceived intelligence and competency.

W.K.Y.S. is an epidemic of massive proportions in the business world that nobody talks about. I cannot tell you how many entrepreneurs and CEOs I have seen stop short of being extraordinary because they are too afraid to leave their definitive lane of validated expertise and widely accepted knowledge. Countless leaders and speakers stop themselves from voicing their significant opinions and monumental concepts to stick with the tips, tricks and formulas they know because of the little voice in the back of their heads wondering if they are qualified to share their ideas. I'm not just referring to young startuppers; I'm also talking about established CEOs of multi-million and billion-dollar companies. Too many people rob the world of their imagination by hiding behind their big corporate brands.

The doubt that creeps up is usually masked in something that sounds quite rational, like: "Well, we don't have enough data," or, "Once we have the success story of going public," or, "When we have a few more customer case studies." Make no mistake, these are all just versions of: "Who am I to say this?" It's Imposter Syndrome rearing its ugly head. So we stick to our field of expertise, cozy up with our credentials, use the industry knowledge we know like the back of our hands, and discuss proven facts and data so we continue to be highly regarded as the serious, intelligent business leaders we are.

We need to get over it. Because that exact vulnerability and "unprovenness" of WHO-WHY is exactly what makes us the unique, thought-provoking, whole-hearted humans we really are. Assume your intelligence and credibility are a given, and get to the good stuff.

W.K.Y.S.

We know you're smart. Stop proving it.

Have the courage to leave what you know for certain in the rearview, step up to the plate, and start taking some hot damn swings.

Even still, W.K.Y.S. is an intellectual fear. It's not scary in your gut like the time my friend Dana hid a human head in my bed. Plastic, but still. It did not go over well.

We all fear something even greater than a human head in our bed that will stop us in our quest to become BIG FISH. Real scary stuff.

Becoming irrelevant.

## CHAPTER 17

# ONE-HIT WONDER

"Never give up, for that is just the place and time
that the tide will turn."

**- HARRIET BEECHER STOWE**

We are scared of firmly planting our WHO-WHY flag and going big on our BIG Idea because we fear putting all our eggs in one basket, losing any possible segment of audience/customer base, and even possibly in the wake of massive success, ultimately becoming a one-hit wonder.

Paradoxically, brands that stay focused on what they do and how they do it are much more likely to become one-hit wonders than BIG FISH focused on their personas and purpose. As we've discussed, WHAT-HOW is rigidly fixed, whereas WHO-WHY is ever-evolving and offers great resilience and ability to pivot.

If you're Blockbuster, your WHAT is videos and your HOW is renting movies to the masses. You can be high and mighty for a time but there's very little place for you to go when Netflix comes in and disrupts your ass.

In contrast, let's circle back to lifestyle guru Tim Ferriss.

Tim Ferriss went big with *The 4-Hour Workweek*. He staked his claim in work productivity. His business was consulting services (WHAT-HOW), but his WHO-WHY was front and center—he was the productivity guy who stood for working less and playing more. His BIG Idea was to devise a system that enables you to work just four hours per week and live like a millionaire.

Cut to a few years later and Tim Ferriss is advising us on meal planning, workouts, how to sleep better, swim faster and have better orgasms. What on earth is the work productivity guy doing teaching us about our bodies? Tim Ferriss evolved the way humans do. He went from being the productivity guy to the max efficiency guy, championing how we can achieve maximum output with the minimum viable dose in every area of our lives.

Look at author Glennon Doyle. She has a spectacular writing career and massive impact as an activist. Oprah named her as one of the world's "awakened leaders who are using their voices and talent to elevate humanity" and author Elizabeth Gilbert thinks she's "the next Gloria Steinem." I've quoted Glennon twice throughout this book because I'm a fangirl. I'm re-reading her memoir *Untamed* for the third time because #fangirl!

The most amazing thing about Glennon Doyle is her unapologetic receptiveness to change. This woman launched her career as a Christian mommy blogger with a memoir about finding her happily-ever-after with her husband and children. Then her husband cheats on her, in real life. Well, shit. She says about it later, "Hell hath no fury like a memoirist whose husband just fucked up her story." But Glennon's story can't get messed up because she is in the fluid waters of WHO. By nature, WHO evolves. Two books later, in *Untamed*, Glennon has left her husband, married a woman, and been excommunicated from the evangelical church. It's her most successful book to date, selling more than 1 million copies in less than 20 weeks. A business rooted in WHAT-HOW would lose everything with that kind of 180. But we recognize that humans change, and so Glennon is able to honor her WHO and take us along with her.

Back to my friend Nick Dawson, the innovation leader in healthcare. Being a truly brilliant human, his curious mind and emerging passions make way for some big WHO-WHY swings, like the time he went from smoking his own bacon and attempting to open source the world of cured meats (he was a straight up meat *cewebrity,* y'all) to becoming a flat out vegan. Our mutual friend lovingly pokes fun and thinks it's nuts to go from one extreme to the other, but I say it's spectacular. People *change.* It's the beauty of being human. We learn new things that shift our perspective and change our minds. It's not weird to change; it's weird to stay the same. Embrace it! Let past beliefs and behaviors fade into the past as you shed that old skin and emerge anew.

There is great resilience in our persona and vision because our WHO and WHY are always evolving. Our personalities grow and our perspectives transform. When we stay in WHAT-HOW, we are stuck within rigid parameters and will become stagnant to the point of irrelevance. In WHO-WHY, we can adapt like ninjas to the ever-changing landscape because our WHO-WHY evolves as we, the humans, evolve.

When I was obsessed with brotivational peak performance, my greatest fear was being average. I made my bed with sharp hospital corners every morning because I knew that it was directly tied to me achieving my goal arbitrary-but-not-average income because how we do anything is how we do everything.

Then I had a newborn and F that stupid bed. Just surviving one hour to the next feeding was a success. And I beat the ever-loving hell out of myself for it because my identity was still Peak Performance Caroline.

One night, I watched *Batman Begins* and a line jumped out and punched me in the gut. In a moment of truth where Batman spares a life out of compassion, the bad guy says, "You lack the courage to do all that is necessary."

If I was committed to doing all that is necessary to succeed and thrive, I would have been side hustling instead of watching *Batman Begins*. I would have opened my laptop instead of sleeping when the baby slept. I would have gone to the gym instead of eating Justin's Dark Chocolate Peanut Butter Cups. I would have poured myself an herbal tea instead of a glass of wine. I would certainly have made my irritating bed.

Did this mean that I did not deserve success?

Modern day success gurus were preaching the need to sacrifice for the bigger picture. We'll never feel like it, but we must do it anyway. Design an environment that forces our success habits. No pain, no gain. Hustle. Grind. Repeat. And I drank the Kool-Aid.

But then in the moment when I realized that I lacked the discipline to do all that is necessary, I wondered, "Is it necessary? Must the struggle be real?"

And just like that, I started questioning what I stood for.

My **WHO-WHY** evolved. I was no longer Peak Performance Caroline. I became Single Mama on a Mission to Thrive Caroline. I launched a YouTube show where my adorable newborn co-host and I gave advice to help single mama entrepreneurs[8]. I wore my baby on stage when I delivered a speech. I made parody videos that juxtaposed the world full of ballers posing in front of private jets with the reality of me singing "Baby Shark" in my Subaru. It became part of everything I did. It was "my thing."

My persona evolved as my life and beliefs evolved. And yours will too. Check in with yourself every few months or after any life change. Is this identity you've personified still you? Are you still passionate about your vision? There is no need to go down with the ship on which we've hoisted our flag if it no longer rings true.

Check in, adjust as needed, and then get right back to going all in.

This brings us to our final and greatest fear of all: our Big, Bad Ego.

[8] If you need a dose of cuteness, check out the 13-episode series on my YouTube channel. I'm partial to the insight I deliver, but who are we kidding, my newborn is a total scene-stealer.

## CHAPTER 18

## BUT...EGO

*"Out of your vulnerabilities will come your strength."*

**- SIGMUND FREUD**

One day back when I was a Hollywood publicist, I was walking through the office when I got whacked in the face by a King Size Snickers bar hurtling through the air with impressive speed. Most people haven't been hit by a candy bar with tremendous force so let me just tell you, it hurts.

I shouted, "OWWW! What the hell?"

One of the publicists called me in from his office and apologized, sort of. He said, "Shit, did that hit you? My bad. Can you move out of the way?"

As I stood aside and rubbed my cheek, he took aim and pelted another one, this time hitting the intended target, his assistant.

That's right. Dude got his jollies from throwing candy bars at his assistant, who was so used to it by this point that he barely flinched upon impact.

Hollywood can be crazy like this because there are a lot of egos, drunk on power, running rampant. Fortunately, most of us do not come close to that level of ego. Still, ego exists in all of us and if we're not aware of its power, it may just pummel us with a Twix.

If you've read this far, you are probably super pumped about embracing your persona and vision. You are ready to lean into your badassery and shout it from the rooftops and your ego is riding high. Or maybe you're the opposite and worried that your ego may go full maniac, so you're slowly retreating into the bushes like that Homer Simpson meme.

Either way, relax. This is where we do a big ol' mindset shift. This is the surprise ending:

Your personal brand platform is not about you. It's about *them*.

People don't actually buy *us*. They buy a better future version of themselves.

Our WHO is not about us. Amplifying our WHO is only to enable our customers to attach to their WHO. It's like a mirror image. They are attracted to something they see in themselves, or more accurately, something they see in their better future version of themselves. I am drawn to Glennon Doyle not because she is Glennon Doyle, but because she has created a life that is so true to who she is and I desire to be that brave. I dream of knowing who I am at the deepest level and writing my own rules for my own life and that is what I'm buying when I buy what Glennon sells.

Same with our WHY. We can go soul searching to tap into our beliefs, purpose and vision, but at the end of the day, it's not about us at all. Amplifying our WHY is only to enable our customers to attach to their WHY. It's like they are going along in their own movie and your WHY simply introduces a new scene, a new vision, and they say, "Hellz yeah! That's where I want to go!" Your WHY activates a vision for a better version of themselves. I am attracted to Annie Grace's point of view on alcohol not because it has anything to do with her purpose, but because I like the idea of being fully present in my own life. I imagine living a vibrant, healthy life that isn't blurred by alcohol and that is what I'm buying when I buy what Annie sells.

By far the most common fear I hear around building personal brand platforms, writing books, speaking or any form of amplifying persona and vision is that it's an ego thing. People feel uncomfortable sharing anything personal because they mistakenly think it's a "hey, look at me" exercise. Please don't go all modest and meek and stay in the safe zone of your professional expertise. When you break free, you simply unleash others.

Make no mistake, when we are leaning into our WHO-WHY, we are out on a limb. Leading with our individual vision can feel like we are standing center stage with a giant spotlight shining on us. We need to lean into the discomfort for the benefit of the collective. We're talking about putting front and center our individual opinions and perspectives not yet supported by endless data and widely accepted best practices of the masses. Of course it will be uncomfortable! In fact, if it's not uncomfortable, we're probably still cozied up in WHAT-HOW.

Everyone hanging out in WHAT-HOW has years of expertise, categorical answers and brand data to wrap around them like Snuggies to make them feel definitively safe and cozy. But we know the truth: Snuggies are lame.

Yet most people stay here in the quicksand of best practices because they are too nervous to speak their WHO-WHY publicly with any kind of amplification necessary for impact because they are concerned it could be perceived as an ego play.

The key to remember when we are all alone out on our limbs is that we are not beating our chests calling ourselves gurus. The greatest thought leaders in the world are constantly curious, learning, changing and adapting. Word is not gospel, it's guidance.

I once heard that it is better to be *interested* than to be *interesting*. I'm a high extrovert but this one little tip changed parties and networking events forever for me. No longer did I have to worry about saying something brilliant that would make people perceive me as interesting. *That* is ego. Instead, I could just be genuinely interested in the conversation.

Our WHO-WHY is not our shiny platform that we stand on to be interesting. It is our contribution to the conversation in which we are genuinely interested.

And now, since we are nearing the end of our time together, it's the perfect place to come full circle back to cults.

CHAPTER 19

# CULT, REVISITED

"With great power comes great responsibility."

**- SPIDER-MAN'S UNCLE**

A word of caution, if I may. This is my public service announcement so I can sleep at night.

The reason that cults are effective is because there is a cult leader who is amplifying the hell out of his WHO-WHY, effectively influencing his followers who are attaching it to their own WHO-WHYS. That's right, the cult leader is a BIG FISH.

So, don't start a cult, okay?

Seriously. Our WHO-WHY is powerful and a great influencer of people. There are many incredible BIG FISH, several of whom we have learned from in this book, who have all used their persona and purpose to grow business, gain revenue, create social impact and build legacies. Bottom line, they have used their WHO-WHY for good. But there are plenty of other BIG FISH who have abused the power. Any charismatic, mission-driven person who has ultimately led people to something false or harmful falls into this category. Elizabeth Holmes. Bernie Madoff. *Hitler.* Anyone on the HBO series *Generation Hustle.* Sadly, these are all examples of BIG FISH too.

Beyond differentiation, we face another monumental challenge today: trust. Or lack thereof. We seem to be at a tipping point of sorts with the public distrust of the media, government and big business. Certainly consumers don't trust our ads or marketing messages. The only way to build trust is via the individual, not the brand. People buy people because people trust people.

I'll say that again: People buy people because people trust people.

Parenting has never been easier because I buy all my crap from just a few people, as most moms I know do. I buy all my daughter's toys from the Melissa & Doug toy line. Every. Single. Toy. I just trust that sweet husband and wife couple, Melissa and Doug. Never mind that they've built a $350 million conglomerate on their dependable faces. They are still Melissa and Doug, married for 30 years, raising six kids. I trust that they're going to give me a sturdy toy that's full of imagination and not lead.

I buy our immunity-boosting elderberry syrup from Taznerda Haley who started the company Black Elder in the South. I don't know her personally, but I trust this person, her story, her mission and, ultimately, the ingredients that she puts in that magical elixir. If some Big Pharma company served me up an Amazon ad for elderberry gummies at half the price, there's no way I'd put that junk in our bodies, because I don't trust Big Pharma.

All our bath and cleaning products are from The Honest Company. I trust that they are good and pure because I trust founder/human Jessica Alba.

All of our food pouches are from Once Upon a Farm. I trust that they are delicious and clean because I trust co-founder/human Jennifer Garner.

Our peanut butter is from Justin's because, Justin. Our bread is from Dave's Killer Bread because, Dave. You get me.

In fact, if I ever have to buy anything outside of what my trusted people sell—like a rando Elsa wig for Halloween—it's a huge pain in the ass. I end up sinking into hours of research on brands, materials and customer reviews. I get thrown into the Sea of Sameness with no floaties. I could make a case for Melissa & Doug selling Everything You Need to Parent, but I can see the can of worms opening to a monopoly, so let's not go there for now.

Trust is real. More than 80% of customers buy based on trust[9]. This goes for different global markets, different ages, and across different income groups. Customers spend 67% more with you when they trust you[10]. Nine in 10 of them will give you a second chance when you screw up and 85% will stick with you when shit hits the fan[11]. Trust makes you more money and saves you the time and hassle of having to constantly replace customers. Of course, it's not just about money. Whenever I sell a customer something—whether it's a $15 book or a $5,000 speech or a $500,000 enterprise solution—it's not about making a buck. It's because I truly believe that the thing they're buying will *help* them. Your success does not make you better; it makes the

[9] Edelman, 2019
[10] CMO, 2020
[11] SproutSocial, 2020

world better. This is about the impact we can have when we move people to action. And that comes from trust.

Our **WHO-WHY** is a trust accelerator. That means it is imperative that we use it for good, to ensure trust is not misplaced. We must be authentic in our persona and genuine in our vision, and not just manufacture them. We must be transparent about where we wish to lead people. This is not some clever marketing gimmick that we spread around like more false information on the internet. That will only create more distrust. We must not only focus on benefiting ourselves and our businesses, but our collective society.

With great power comes great responsibility. There is true power in becoming a BIG FISH and it is a conscious choice to use this newfound power for good.

Remember this moment. May it be the moment you step out of your career conditioning and into your human potential.

## CHAPTER 20

# SWIM FORTH, BIG FISH

*"You are a goddamn cheetah."*

**- GLENNON DOYLE**

I cried in the car the other day. A familiar song with sappy lyrics took me down hard. I remembered back to college graduation and how much my mom loved the tune:

> *I hope you never fear those mountains in the distance,*
> *Never settle for the path of least resistance,*
> *And when you get the choice to sit it out or dance,*
> *I hope you dance.*

There it was. What once stood in all of its wide-eyed, bushy-tailed glory: Potential.

We're raised to believe in our potential. We are all unique and have special gifts that will change the world. We can do anything. But as I get older, I look around and mainly see everyone on the path of normalcy, only now they're looking down at their children saying, "You can do anything."

In a world that seems to value square pegs fitting neatly into square holes, are we just passing potential from generation to generation?

"There is one place that all the people with the greatest potential are gathered and that's the graveyard," Viola Davis said in her acceptance speech for Best Supporting Actress at the 2016 Academy Awards. "I say exhume those bodies. Exhume those stories—the stories of the people who dreamed big and never saw those dreams to fruition."

Is reaching our potential a metaphoric mountaintop that's always going to be in the distance? Are we getting any closer with our CRMs, SQLs, editorial calendars and WHAT-HOW footsteps? I have a good life and career, but can I really say that I am living out my maximum potential and creating a legacy core to my being?

Can you?

Life is short. It shocks me how we meander along, day in and day out, following the status quo like zombies in smart business casual.

Now I know you, dear reader, are not a cog in a machine. You are an entrepreneur, an ambitious business leader, but as long as we continue to stay in the land of WHAT-HOW, we are squandering our potential in this one glorious life. WHAT-HOW robs the world of our individual, unique gifts.

The planet doesn't need another widget. The planet desperately needs more critical thinkers, passionate leaders and mission-driven visionaries of all kinds. So says the Dalai Lama (ish).

What do we know? We know our world has changed to the point where we cannot possibly sustain in business as long as we promote **WHAT** we do and **HOW** we do it. We know we must define our **WHO** and claim our **WHY** with a BIG Idea to become BIG FISH. Through the many examples in this book, we have seen how this strategy of leading with **WHO-WHY** massively differentiates us and creates raving fans to drive big revenue to our businesses.

But we also know that being a BIG FISH is about so much more than driving revenue. BIGFISHdom creates true impact. People are not just spending more money with us; their lives are being shaped in some capacity by our persona and vision. We are shifting people's perspectives. We are leading new thought, influencing mindsets and changing human behavior to alter life's trajectory. You are no longer just growing a business behind a brand, but making a dent with your one-and-only-in-the-history-of-the-world self. And that—that right there—is legacy.

Get out there and show the world who you are.

Share your vision. Evangelize your BIG Idea.

Swim forth, BIG FISH. It's time to make waves.

## GRATITUDE

This book would not exist without the following people, for whom I am truly grateful.

*Andrew Davis,* for much of the thinking that showed up in these pages, for everything I know about BIG Ideas and frameworks, and for always believing in my potential and making me better. My career is infinitely greater and more fun with you in it.

*Carter Dandridge,* for being the feet on the ground to my head in the clouds (and by that of course I mean forcing me to write literal explanations when all I want to write is metaphors). You are my favorite editor in the whole wide world.

*Justin Harris,* for your design brilliance. We have collaborated now for more than a decade. My words would feel stark naked without you.

*Kip Bulwinkle,* for your exuberance and the greatest name ever. Thank you for capturing me through each changing season of life.

*Hunter Nuttall,* for instantly agreeing to meticulously proofread your baby sister's book, even at the "friends and family rate."

*Bree Barton,* for your enthusiastic help when I was asked for my book proposal and had to Google "what is a book proposal."

*Olivia Leonard,* for the "poodle about to be thrown into a bathtub" one-liner (oh, and for being my dear friend and godmother to my only child).

*Mom,* for calling me in tears after you read my book proposal and simply saying, "*Caroline, you are a writer.*" Your confidence in me is everything.

*Dad,* for keeping Mom calm when she reads my sometimes salty language and reference to "poop baby" in Chapter 5.

*Coco,* for entertaining yourself with oodles of playdough while Mommy wrote this book. We did this side by side, baby girl.

And finally, I am grateful to *all my friends and family* for listening to my incessant thoughts, opinions and ideas of how to make the world better.

## ABOUT THE AUTHOR

Caroline G. Nuttall is an author and speaker. As well as founding, building, and selling a successful multimedia company, Caroline was a Hollywood publicist for some of the world's biggest and most beloved brands. She went on to serve as a Vice President at ForbesBooks and CEO of the world's first talent agency for marketing thought leaders. Today, Caroline develops leaders and helps transform organizations. She lives in Charleston, South Carolina, with her daughter, Coco.

CAROLINE@BIGFISH.LIFE

CNUTTALL

CPSIA information can be obtained
at www.ICGtesting.com
Printed in the USA
BVHW061119140222
628967BV00004B/179